THE 5-INGREDIENT TYPE 2 DIABETES COOKBOOK

800 Days 5-Ingredient Recipes for Living Well with Type 2 Diabetes. (21-Day Meal Plan for Beginners)

Juanita J. Dunn

Text & Photographs Copyright © 2021 by Juanita J. Dunn

All rights reserved, Published in the United States.

Disclaimer: The information contained in this book is based on the experience and research of the author. It is not intended as a substitute for consulting with your physician or other health-care provider. Any attempt to diagnose and treat an illness should be done under the direction of a health-care professional. The publisher and author are not responsible for any adverse effects or consequences resulting from the use of any of the suggestions, preparations, or procedures discussed in this book.

Some of the recipes in this book include raw eggs, meat, or fish. When these foods are consumed raw, there is always the risk that bacteria, which is killed by proper cooking, may be present. For this reason, when se1ving these foods raw, always buy certified salmonella -free eggs and the freshest n1eat and fish available fron1a reliable grocer, storing them in the refrigerator until they are se1ved. Because of the health risks associated with the consumption of bacteria that can be present in raw eggs, meat, and fish, these foods should not be consumed by infants, small children, pregnant women, the elderly, or any persons who may be immunocompromised. The author and publisher expressly disclaim responsibility for any adverse effects that may result from the use or application of the recipes and information contained in this book.

TABLE OF CONTENTS

KNOW THE TYPE 2 DIABETES 5
EATING RIGHT: FINDING YOUR WAY WITH THE FOOD GROUPS 7
MAKE THE MOST OF YOUR MEALS 9
STOCKING A DIABETES-FRIENDLY KITCHEN 13

21-DAY MEAL PLAN 17

BREAKFAST RECIPES 19
Sausage Potato Skillet Casserole 19
Almond Quinoa With Cranberries 20
Sweet Onion Frittata With Ham 21
Spinach And Feta Omelets 22
Busy Day Breakfast Burrito 23
Kale Chips 24
Cheesy Mushroom Omelet 25
Double-Duty Banana Pancakes 26
Raisin French Toast With Apricot Spread 27
Strawberry-Carrot Smoothies 28
Breakfast Grilled Swiss Cheese And Rye 29
English Muffin Melts 30
Peach Cranberry Quick Bread 31
Orange-Honey Yogurt 32

VEGETARIAN RECIPES 33
Black Bean And Corn Bowl 33
Cauliflower Steaks With Chimichurri Sauce 34
"Refried" Bean And Rice Casserole 35
Pesto Potatoes And Edamame Bake 36
Hurried Hummus Wraps 37
Speedy Greek Orzo Salad 38
Tomato Topper Over Anything 39
Skillet-Grilled Meatless Burgers With Spicy Sour Cream 40
Feta Basil Pasta 41
Toasted Grain And Arugula 41
Open-Faced Grilled Pepper-Goat Cheese Sandwiches 42
Cheesy Tortilla Rounds 43

SALADS RECIPES 44
Zesty Citrus Melon 44
Toasted Pecan And Apple Salad 44
Seaside Shrimp Salad 45
Caesar'd Chicken Salad 46
Tangy Sweet Carrot Pepper Salad 46
Feta'd Tuna With Greens 47
Bibb Lettuce Salad With Endive & Cucumber .. 48
Creamy Dill Cucumbers 48
Ginger'd Ambrosia 49
Orange Pomegranate Salad With Honey 49
Minted Carrot Salad 50
Mesclun Salad With Goat Cheese & Almonds .. 51
Carrot Cranberry Matchstick Salad 51
Crispy Crunch Coleslaw 52

MEAT RECIPES 53
Sweet Jerk Pork 53
Country-Style Ham And Potato Casserole 54
Grapefruit-Zested Pork 55
Zesty Beef Patties With Grilled Onions 56
Pork With Tomato Caper Sauce 57
Homestyle Double-Onion Roast 58
Grilled Dijon Pork Roast 59
Spicy Chili'd Sirloin Steak 59
Sizzling Pork Chops 60

Sausage Pilaf Peppers 61
Chili-Stuffed Potatoes 61
Easy & Elegant Tenderloin Roast 62
Sriracha-Roasted Pork With Sweet Potatoes 63
Beef Strips With Sweet Ginger Sauce 64

POULTRY RECIPES 65
Taco Chicken Tenders 65
Chicken Sausage&Onion Smothered Grits 65
Hoisin Chicken 66
Greek Chicken With Lemon 67
Sausage And Farro Mushrooms 68
Avocado And Green Chili Chicken 68
Cheesy Chicken And Rice 69
Peach Barbecued Chicken 70
Panko Ranch Chicken Strips With Dipping Sauce 71
Molasses Drumsticks With Soy Sauce 71
Turkey Patties With Dark Onion Gravy 72
In-a-Pinch Chicken & Spinach 73
Turkey & Apricot Wraps 74
Rustic Mexican Chicken And Rice 74

APPETIZERS AND SNACKS 75
Mocha Pumpkin Seeds 75
Basil Spread And Water Crackers 75
Crostini With Kalamata Tomato 76
Lime'd Blueberries 77
Bleu Cheese'd Pears 77
Tuna Salad Stuffed Eggs 78
Dilled Chex Toss 79
Creamy Apricot Fruit Dip 79
Minutesi Feta Pizzas 80

Balsamic-Goat Cheese Grilled Plums 80
Sweet Peanut Buttery Dip 81
Baby Carrots And Spicy Cream Dip 82

FISH & SEAFOOD RECIPES 83
Two-Sauce Cajun Fish 83
Pesto Grilled Salmon 84
Shrimp And Noodles Parmesan 85
Lemony Steamed Spa Fish 86
Salmon With Lemon-Thyme Slices 87
Pan-Seared Sesame-Crusted Tuna Steaks 88
Buttery Lemon Grilled Fish 89
Teriyaki Salmon 90
No-Fry Fish Fry 91
Oven-Roasted Salmon 92

VEGETABLES, FRUIT &SIDE DISHES.. 93
Roasted Spiralized Carrots 93
Creole-Simmered Vegetables 94
Saucy Eggplant And Capers 95
Roasted Beets 96
Roasted Beans And Green Onions 97
Best Baked Sweet Potatoes 98
Buttery Tarragon Sugar Snaps 99
Light Glazed Skillet Apples 99
Pan-Roasted Broccoli 100
Roasted Asparagus 101
Slow-Cooked Whole Carrots 102
Grilled Soy Pepper Petites 103
Hot Skillet Pineapple 104
Broccoli Piquant 105
Skillet-Roasted Veggies 106

INTRODUCTION

KNOW THE TYPE 2 DIABETES

Types of Diabetes

Just as the causes of diabetes greatly vary, its types also vary, and each type is treated and controlled differently. If the cause is insulin resistance, you can not treat it by injecting more insulin. For that, you would need some other measures. So it is essential to know which type of diabetes you are suffering from. Here are the three types of diabetes:

1. Type I:

This type of diabetes is the result of the body's own autoimmune response. It means that our defense mechanism damages the pancreatic cells that produce insulin. As a result, our pancreas stops producing insulin or start producing them in an insufficient amount. This type of diabetes can happen at any time of your age, irrespective of your gender and the gene type. People suffering from diabetes type I need insulin to be injected artificially on day to day basis in order to maintain levels of glucose in their blood. They also can take insulin orally, but that it is usually not as effective as the direct injections.

2. Type II:

90% of diabetic patients suffer from this type of diabetes. It is mostly diagnosed in people of adults ages, but today, young adults are also equally susceptible to the disease. This type of diabetes can stay undetected for several years as it can only be identified through special tests. Good diet and constant exercise can only control the harms of this diabetes. The patient may require some extra dose of insulin both orally or through injections. It is also known as the 'Prediabetes,' and it is caused due to the inability of the body to respond to the insulin production in the body. There is no apparent damage to the cells producing the insulin unlike type I diabetes.

3. Gestational Diabetes (GDM)

As the name indicates it, this type of diabetes can occur to a mother during the gestational period or pregnancy. The good news is that it is not permanent but a temporary condition and persists only during the pregnancy. It is caused by the production of certain hormones from the placenta of the baby, and these hormones can disrupt the functioning of the insulin. So the body becomes insulin resistant. It is not always harmful, but the condition can get critical in case of malnutrition or poor dietary intake.

Three Myths Worth Busting

1. People with diabetes have to eat different meals and snacks from the rest of the family.

It's true that family members with diabetes have to watch what they eat, but there's no need to cook separate dishes. Everyone will benefit from eating more leafy greens, high-fiber foods and lean proteins.

2. People with diabetes can't eat sweets or desserts.

Almost everyone has a hankering for something sweet from time to time. A good way to deal with a food craving is to enjoy a little taste. Having a small portion on special occasions will prevent you from feeling deprived so you can keep focusing on healthful foods.

3. People with diabetes shouldn't eat starchy foods.

Everyone needs carbohydrates for energy. Whole grains and starchy vegetables like potatoes, yams, peas and corn can be included in meals and snacks, but portion size is key. According to the American Diabetes Association, a good place to start is to aim for 45-60 grams of carbohydrate per meal or 3-4 servings per day of carbohydrate-containing foods. Depending on your needs and how you manage your diabetes, you may need to adjust this amount. Your health care team can help you determine suitable portions.

Quick Facts from the American Diabetes Association

- Twenty-nine million Americans have Type 2 diabetes and about 86 million have prediabetes—and the number is rising.
- Type 2 diabetes accounts for 90 to 95 percent of all cases of diabetes.
- Eating well and losing even a few pounds can reduce the risk of diabetes and other health problems.

EATING RIGHT: FINDING YOUR WAY WITH THE FOOD GROUPS

You've been taught about the four basic food groups since childhood, and may be wondering how they fit into this diabetes equation. Here's the run down:

1. Fruits and Vegetables.

Filled with nutrients and good for you, fruits and veggies are definitely part of a healthy "diabetes diet." Dark leafy green veggies that are high in fiber are best, while starchy vegetables like potatoes should be eaten in moderation. Good low-carb choices include broccoli, green beans, spinach, kale, green peppers, asparagus, okra, cauliflower, and lettuce.

Fruits contain natural sugars (fructose) that raise blood sugar levels, so choose ones that are high in fiber to moderate that effect. Watermelon, strawberries, grapefruit, blackberries, blueberries, honeydew melon, and avocado (yes, it's a fruit) are all choices that should be kind to your blood sugar levels. Like veggies, no fruits are off-limits, but those that are higher in carbs, like bananas, figs, mangoes, and grapes, should be eaten in small portions. And remember that all dried fruits (e.g., raisins, prunes, dates, dried apricots) are extremely high in sugar.

2. Breads and Cereals.

This is a tricky category. It's important to get some whole grains in your diet to promote good diabetes and heart health. Yet breads and cereals tend to be very high in carbohydrates and therefore not a great choice for keeping blood sugars steady. Checking the label is important. There should be at least 5 g of fiber, if not more, in a serving. Look at the nutrition facts panel for total carbohydrates as well, and comparison shop for a bread that has more fiber and fewer carbs. Avoid cereal products that contain sweeteners like high fructose corn syrup and even sugar, molasses, and honey. It's better for your blood sugar if you add your own sweetener, or a low-carb fruit, to an unsweetened cereal.

3. Dairy.

Both the ADA and the USDA recommend low-fat versus full-fat dairy products. Traditionally this recommendation has been based on the presumed link between saturated fat and heart disease.

However, recent research, including a 2010 meta-analysis of twenty-one studies and nearly 350,000 subjects, has found that dietary saturated fat was not associated with an increased risk of coronary heart or vascular disease.

Whether or not saturated fat is the dietary culprit it has long believed to have been is a subject of hot debate in the nutrition world, and it will probably continue to be for some time. If your doctor, diabetes educator, or dietitian does recommend low-fat dairy to you, just keep in mind that low-fat food products often have added carbohydrates in the form of sugars or thickeners to improve their taste. As always, check the label for total carbohydrates and adjust your serving sizes accordingly.

4. Meat, Poultry, and Fish (Protein).

When prepared without sauces or breading, meat, poultry, and fish are all carbohydrate free. Choosing lean cuts of meat will help you avoid some of the added fat and calories. The ADA recommends two or more servings of fish a week for the heart-healthy omega-3 fatty acids it provides.

Even if you follow your meal plan to the letter, you're still going to find that certain foods will give you a bigger spike in blood sugar levels than expected. You may also find that other foods you expected to pump up your readings barely bump the meter. That's the individual nature of diabetes. For this reason, a food diary is an invaluable tool in figuring out just how different foods affect your blood glucose levels.

As you learn how variations in food choices, timing of meals, and exercise affect your blood glucose levels, you and your dietitian and doctor can work together to fine-tune your carb-counting program. It is a learning process, so don't be disappointed if it doesn't fall into place immediately.

Record the type, amount, and timing of foods eaten, along with what effect they had on your blood sugar levels (a reading before eating and a reading two hours after). Many people choose to record the information in a blood sugar logbook. At first it may feel a little obsessive-compulsive to chronicle every bite, but you'll find it's worth it when the time comes to figure out a mysterious high or an unexpected low. It's also a great cure for mindless eating—you won't thoughtlessly polish off what the kids left on their dinner plate or munch samples in the supermarket if you've trained yourself to write it down.

INTRODUCTION

MAKE THE MOST OF YOUR MEALS

1. Breakfast

Cereal. Toast. Cereal. Toast. It can get pretty monotonous. Get out of your rut! Take a new approach toward the breakfast meal and what it has to offer.

With our multitasking day and night, why not set the breakfast meal to multitasking, too? Serve these tasty recipes not only for breakfast, but also for lunch, midday snack, dinner, and even dessert.

Or take a look in the other chapters, such as Beverages or Snacks, and see what would work for a breakfast item. Just choose the recipes to fit your inclinations, while keeping track of your carb intake. I designed these recipes to be versatile enough to fit into other parts of your day as well, giving you even more choices for each meal.

Breakfast Tricks, Tips, and Timesavers

1. Bake a batch. Muffins or quick breads are perfect for breakfast for one day and a snack or dessert the next. Then freeze the rest in small baggies and pull them out when you need them.

2. Breakfast power drinks. You can make the beverage recipes in this chapter in just a few minutes, making them great additions to your "on the run" meal or "computer" lunch. Since you need power all day, why not feel as though you're having a treat while you're at it?

3. Double-time your meals. Make a batch of breakfast-grilled sandwiches, have one for breakfast, and refrigerate the rest. Pop one into the microwave at work or home the next day for a quick "already-made" lunch.

4. Add a veggie or salad. For dinner, all you need is to steam a few vegetables and toss a fruit salad to transform an omelet or frittata into a fast-fixing dinner option.

5. Reverse it. Make a fruit drink from the Beverage chapter for breakfast. A fruit drink has fruit juices, fruit, and sometimes yogurt in it, making one a fun and easy part of your breakfast! Or how about using the skillet-grilled fruit in the Fruit Sides chapter to serve alongside your turkey sausage or Canadian bacon in the morning. It's easy to expand your menu once you start thinking out of the breakfast box.

2. Main Dishes

Seasonings play a very important part in main dishes. It's important how and when you use them. To get the most flavor from your meats and casseroles, sometimes you need to season before you start to cook, and other times, after. Check the tips below for some great seasoning ideas.

Main Dish Tricks, Tips, and Timesavers

1. Season with the skin on. Season a chicken or turkey that will be cooked with the skin on by lifting up the skin and rubbing the seasonings between the meat and the skin. Then roast the bird. The seasonings will penetrate into the meat of the bird rather than get lost in the skin that is discarded.

2. Check the label. Some brands of turkey breast and pork tenderloin have broth or solution added, which means added sodium. Be sure to read the package labels, and if the turkey or pork does contain broth or solution, don't add more salt when cooking it.

3. Use coffee granules. If you haven't tried using coffee to intensify the hearty flavor of beef, you'll be amazed! Just add 1/2 cup of strong coffee to the roasting pan and pop it in the oven. Or use instant coffee granules dissolved in water. And you don't need to heat the liquid first—the granules dissolve in either hot or cold liquid. Just be sure to stir them well.

4. Deepen the color. To give a deeper brown appearance to pork, beef, poultry, or fish, dust with a small amount of paprika or chili powder before cooking. Just a light sprinkle will give more color than flavor.

5. Crush those herbs. Dried herbs take a longer time to release their flavors than fresh or ground varieties, so crush the dried herb leaves between your fingertips before adding them to the dish. Fresh herb flavors are strong, but they fade quickly if cooked for a long time.

6. Use citrus zest and juice. When a recipe calls for both the zest and juice of a lemon, lime, or orange, always grate the piece of fruit first before squeezing the juice out. It's easier to grate when the fruit is full and firm. Grate only the colorful part of the fruit, not the white pith underneath—that gives the dish a bitter taste.

INTRODUCTION

Main Dish Tricks, Tips, and Timesavers After You Start Cooking

1.   Add ground spices. If you need a stronger, more intense flavor in a dish, add ground spices after cooking. You just need a small amount, and the flavor doesn't break down while cooking.

2.   Use a smidgen of sugar. Add small amounts (1/2 to 1 teaspoon) to stews and skillet dishes. It doesn't add sweetness to the dish, but aids in cutting the acidity of the other ingredients and acts to blend the flavors together.

3.   A so-simple sauce. Reduction is a fancy word for boiling down the liquid in a dish quickly to leave a deeply flavored, intense sauce. This is my favorite cooking trick. Simply add water, broth, or wine to the skillet after sautéing other ingredients. The liquid will absorb the concentrated seasonings that build up in the skillet during the cooking process, then boil down in 1 or 2 minutes to create a quick, highly flavored sauce.

4.   Last-minute flavors. Add the following ingredients to your dishes once they have been removed from the heat. These can also be added to cold entrees at serving time.
- Extracts, such as vanilla and almond extract
- Grated citrus rind and gingerroot
- Flavored oils, such as extra virgin olive oil and sesame oil
- Toasted nuts

3. Vegetable Sides

Night after night of boiled frozen veggies, or heated canned ones, can get really tiresome. The recipes here let you see how easy, interesting, and sensational veggie and fruit sides can be. By preparing them in a variety of ways—roasted, steamed, stuffed, mixed with other vegetables, skillet-grilled, and more—you'll look at vegetable sides in a different light . . . and find some new favorites.

Vegetable Tricks, Tips, and Timesavers

1. Line it with foil. When roasting vegetables, always line the baking sheet with foil to protect the baking sheet surface and give you easy clean-up.

2. Maximize your buttery taste. To get the most concentrated "butter" flavors from light margarine—whether you boil, steam, or roast the veggies—add it after cooking, not during. And don't worry about melting light margarine first—just place it directly on the veggies and let their heat melt it. The flavor of light margarine is so much better that way.

3. The right cut. How you cut a vegetable is important, so be sure to follow the recipe's instructions. Veggie cut affects the evenness of cooking, cooking time, and recipe presentation, so follow directions to be successful!

STOCKING A DIABETES-FRIENDLY KITCHEN

We use a lot of familiar ingredients in our recipes, but reach for their lower salt and sometimes lower-fat versions in order to meet our nutritional guidelines. That means using no-salt-added or unsalted store-bought products like broth, beans, and tomatoes and some low-fat dairy products (milk, yogurt, and sour cream). To increase the amount of protein and fiber while keeping empty calories in check, we call for 100 percent whole-wheat bread and pasta, more white than red meats, and more whole grains and non-starchy vegetables.

1. No-salt-added Products

The convenience of buying commercial items at the supermarket can't be beat; but that convenience can come with a high-sodium price tag. That's why we call for no-salt-added canned ingredients in the recipes in this book.

1. **Unsalted Chicken Broth:** Unsalted means that no salt was added during processing. Even so, unsalted broth still contains sodium. Our winning unsalted broth is Swanson Unsalted Chicken Stock, which has subtle but distinct chicken flavor.

2. **Unsalted Vegetable Broth:** Double-check the nutrition label since unsalted vegetable broths still have quite a bit of naturally occurring sodium. Look for a broth that lists vegetable content first on the ingredient list. We used Edward & Sons Low Sodium Not-Chick'n Bouillon Cubes when testing our recipes.

3. **No-salt-added Canned Beans:** (chickpeas, black beans, cannellini beans, pinto beans, etc.) Beans are a great source of fiber. Canned beans are made by pressure-cooking dried beans directly in the can with water, salt, and preservatives. That is why it's important to use canned beans that were processed without any added salt. We had good luck using canned beans from Eden Organics.

4. **No-salt-added Canned Tomatoes**: Canned tomatoes are processed at the height of freshness so they deliver better flavor than off-season fresh tomatoes. We call for no-salt-added diced, crushed, and whole peeled tomatoes as well as tomato paste. We used Hunt's brand no-salt-added tomato products when testing the recipes.

5. **Natural Peanut Butter**: Peanut butter (and other nut butters) is a convenient source of both protein and healthy fats. Be sure to look for nut butters with no salt or sugar added.

2. Flavor Boosters

We aimed to limit our use of salt in the recipes in the book. Since salt is a flavor enhancer, we found creative ways to replace it. In addition to creating flavor with aromatics like garlic, ginger, and fresh herbs and acidic ingredients like citrus and vinegar, we employed bolder-flavored spices and seasonings.

1. **Bold Spices**: We reach into the spice rack for high-performance spices like bay leaves, cumin, curry, cayenne, smoked paprika, and za'atar.

2. **Super-flavorful Seasonings**: We use very small amounts of high-test ingredients like these to help build great flavor: Dijon mustard, capers, low-sodium soy sauce, and sun-dried tomatoes.

3. Heart-healthy Oils

Plant-based oils are rich in either mono- or polyunsaturated fats (or both) and are a good choice for a diabetic diet. Cold-pressed or expeller-pressed oils are more nutritious because they retain more of their antioxidants but they spoil more quickly and have lower smoking points.

1. **Extra-virgin Olive Oil**: Extra-virgin olive oil is high in healthy fats (monounsaturated fatty acids) as well as antioxidants. Studies have shown that people who regularly include olive oil in

their diet have reduced rates of diabetes. Our winning supermarket EVOO is California Olive Ranch Everyday Extra Virgin Olive Oil.

2. **Canola Oil**: This vegetable oil has become a kitchen standard. It comes from rapeseed plants that have been bred to have a neutral taste and are a good source of plant omega-3s.

3. **Mayonnaise**: Full-fat mayo is actually loaded with healthy fats; it has the same ratio of unsaturated to saturated fats as avocado. Our winner is Blue Plate Mayonnaise.

4. **Light Coconut Milk**: We use light coconut milk when developing our recipes because it has less saturated fat than full-fat coconut milk. The light version still adds plenty of rich flavor and body. We like using Thai Kitchen Lite Coconut Milk in the test kitchen.

4. Whole Grains

Whole grains are often less processed and contain both bran and germ. This means that they contain more fiber and nutrients and so are a healthier choice than their white counterparts.

1. **Brown Rice**: Brown rice is whole-grain, gluten-free, and inexpensive. It is less processed than white rice so it has more fiber, although it still can be digested rapidly and should be eaten in moderation. We only use brown rice in the book. Our winning brand is Lundberg Organic Brown Long Grain Rice.

2. **Bulgur**: Bulgur is a highly nutritious grain made from partially cooked wheat berries that are dried and only partially stripped of their outer bran layer.

3. **Farro**: **Farro** is hulled whole-wheat kernels.

4. **Wheat Berries**: Wheat berries are whole, unprocessed kernels of wheat. They are an excellent source of nutrition because none of the grain has been removed.

5. 100 Percent Whole-wheat Bread and Pasta

Because it includes the bran and germ, whole-wheat flour contains proteins, fats, fiber, vitamins, and minerals that refined white flour lacks.

1. **100 Percent Whole-wheat Bread**: Whole-wheat bread has a flavor and nutrient profile more complex than that of white bread. Our winner is Arnold Whole Grains 100% Whole Wheat Bread.

2. **100 Percent Whole-wheat Pasta:** Made from 100-percent whole durum wheat, whole-wheat pasta has more protein and fiber than the best white pastas. Our winner is Bionaturae Organic 100% Whole Wheat Spaghetti.

6. Dairy Products

Dairy products are a great way to get high-quality protein into a recipe.

1. **Low-fat Milk, Yogurt, and Sour Cream**: We use low-fat versions of these to help us keep within our nutritional guidelines for saturated fat.

2. **Full-fat Cheese, Cottage Cheese, Cream Cheese , and Ricotta Cheese**: We use the full-fat versions of these because we like their flavor better. Most hard cheeses are also fermented, and cheeses and other fermented foods are also increasingly linked to lower risk of diabetes.

INTRODUCTION

21-DAY MEAL PLAN

Meal Plan	Breakfast	Lunch	Dinner
Day-1	Sausage Potato Skillet Casserole	Cauliflower Steaks With Chimichurri Sauce	Caesar'd Chicken Salad
Day-2	Almond Quinoa With Cranberries	Refried" Bean And Rice Casserole	Roasted Beans And Green Onions
Day-3	Sweet Onion Frittata With Ham	Skillet-Grilled Meatless Burgers With Spicy Sour Cream	Sausage Pilaf Peppers
Day-4	Spinach And Feta Omelets	Sweet Jerk Pork	Pesto Potatoes And Edamame Bake
Day-5	Busy Day Breakfast Burrito	Country-Style Ham And Potato Casserole	Easy & Elegant Tenderloin Roast
Day-6	Kale Chips	Grapefruit-Zested Pork	Beef Strips With Sweet Ginger Sauce
Day-7	Cheesy Mushroom Omelet	Oven-Roasted Salmon	Zesty Beef Patties With Grilled Onions
Day-8	Double-Duty Banana Pancakes	No-Fry Fish Fry	Cheesy Chicken And Rice
Day-9	Raisin French Toast With Apricot Spread	Pork With Tomato Caper Sauce	Panko Ranch Chicken Strips With Dipping Sauce
Day-10	Strawberry-Carrot Smoothies	Teriyaki Salmon	Homestyle Double-Onion Roast

Day-11	Breakfast Grilled Swiss Cheese And Rye	Grilled Dijon Pork Roast	Creamy Dill Cucumbers
Day-12	English Muffin Melts	Spicy Chili'd Sirloin Steak	Shrimp And Noodles Parmesan
Day-13	Peach Cranberry Quick Bread	Buttery Lemon Grilled Fish On Grilled Asparagus	Grilled Soy Pepper Petites
Day-14	Orange-Honey Yogurt	Pesto Grilled Salmon	Hot Skillet Pineapple
Day-15	Black Bean And Corn Bowl	Two-Sauce Cajun Fish	Bibb Lettuce Salad With Endive And Cucumber
Day-16	Open-Faced Grilled Pepper-Goat Cheese Sandwiches	Turkey Patties With Dark Onion Gravy	Feta'd Tuna With Greens
Day-17	Cheesy Tortilla Rounds	Pan-Seared Sesame-Crusted Tuna Steaks	Broccoli Piquant
Day-18	Toasted Grain And Arugula	Hoisin Chicken	Zesty Citrus Melon
Day-19	Speedy Greek Orzo Salad	Greek Chicken With Lemon	Tangy Sweet Carrot Pepper Salad
Day-20	Toasted Pecan And Apple Salad	Salmon With Lemon-Thyme Slices	Skillet-Roasted Veggies
Day-21	Crostini With Kalamata Tomato	Rustic Mexican Chicken And Rice	Seaside Shrimp Salad

BREAKFAST RECIPES

Sausage Potato Skillet Casserole

Servings: 4
Cooking Time: 17 Minutes

Ingredients:
- 5 ounces reduced-fat, smoked turkey sausage, kielbasa style
- 2 cups chopped onion
- 4 cups frozen hash brown potatoes with peppers and onions
- 1/3 cup shredded, reduced-fat, sharp cheddar cheese

Directions:
1. Cut the sausage in fourths lengthwise. Cut each piece of sausage in 1/4-inch pieces.
2. Place a large nonstick skillet over medium-high heat until hot. Coat the skillet with nonstick cooking spray, add sausage, and cook 3 minutes or until the sausage begins to brown, stirring frequently. Set the sausage aside on a separate plate.
3. Recoat the skillet with nonstick cooking spray, add the onions, and cook 5 minutes or until the onions begin to brown, stirring frequently.
4. Reduce the heat to medium, add the frozen potatoes and sausage, and cook 9 minutes or until the potatoes are lightly browned, stirring occasionally.
5. Remove the skillet from the heat, top with cheese, cover, and let stand 5 minutes to melt the cheese and develop flavors.

Nutrition Info: 190 cal., 5g fat (2g sag. fat), 25mg chol, 450mg sod., 26g carb (5g sugars, 4g fiber), 9g pro.

Almond Quinoa With Cranberries

Servings: 4

Cooking Time: 17 Minutes

Ingredients:
- 4 ounces slivered almonds
- 3/4 cup dry quinoa
- 3 tablespoons dried cranberries
- 1 tablespoon honey (or 1 tablespoon cinnamon sugar)

Directions:

1. Heat a large saucepan over medium-high heat. Add almonds and cook 2 minutes or until beginning to lightly brown, stirring frequently. Set aside on separate plate.

2. Pour 1 1/2 cups water into the saucepan and bring to a boil, add the quinoa, reduce heat to low, cover and cook 13–15 minutes or until liquid is absorbed. Remove from heat and let stand, covered, for 5 minutes.

3. Top with the almonds and cranberries. Drizzle with the honey (or sprinkle with cinnamon sugar.)

Nutrition Info: 330 cal., 16g fat (1g sag. fat), 0mg chol, 0mg sod., 39g carb (12g sugars, 6g fiber), 11g pro.

Sweet Onion Frittata With Ham

Servings: 4

Cooking Time: 8 Minutes

Ingredients:

- 4 ounces extra-lean, low-sodium ham slices, chopped
- 1 cup thinly sliced Vidalia onion
- 1 1/2 cups egg substitute
- 1/3 cup shredded, reduced-fat, sharp cheddar cheese

Directions:

1. Place a medium nonstick skillet over medium-high heat until hot. Coat the skillet with nonstick cooking spray, add ham, and cook until beginning to lightly brown, about 2–3 minutes, stirring frequently. Remove from skillet and set aside on separate plate.

2. Reduce the heat to medium, coat the skillet with nonstick cooking spray, add onions, and cook 4 minutes or until beginning to turn golden, stirring frequently.

3. Reduce the heat to medium low, add ham to the onions, and cook 1 minute (this allows the flavors to blend and the skillet to cool slightly before the eggs are added). Pour egg substitute evenly over all, cover, and cook 8 minutes or until puffy and set.

4. Remove the skillet from the heat, sprinkle cheese evenly over all, cover, and let stand 3 minutes to melt the cheese and develop flavors.

Nutrition Info: 110 cal., 2g fat (1g sag. fat), 20mg chol, 460mg sod., 6g carb (4g sugars, 0g fiber), 17g pro.

BREAKFAST RECIPES

Spinach And Feta Omelets

Servings: 2

Cooking Time: 10 Minutes

Ingredients:

- 4 large eggs
- 1 tablespoon canola oil
- 1 shallot, minced
- 4 ounces (4 cups) baby spinach
- 1 ounce feta cheese, crumbled (¼ cup)

Directions:

1. Beat 2 eggs with fork in bowl until eggs are thoroughly combined and color is pure yellow; do not overbeat. Repeat with remaining 2 eggs in second bowl.

2. Heat 1 teaspoon oil in 10-inch nonstick skillet over medium heat until shimmering. Add shallot and cook until softened, about 2 minutes. Stir in spinach and cook until wilted, about 1 minute. Using tongs, squeeze out any excess moisture from spinach mixture, then transfer to bowl and cover to keep warm. Wipe skillet clean with paper towels and let cool slightly.

3. Heat 1 teaspoon oil in now-empty skillet over medium heat until shimmering. Add 1 bowl of eggs and cook until edges begin to set, 2 to 3 seconds. Using rubber spatula, stir eggs in circular motion until slightly thickened, about 10 seconds. Use spatula to pull cooked edges of eggs in toward center, then tilt skillet to 1 side so that uncooked eggs run to edge of skillet. Repeat until omelet is just set but still moist on surface, 20 to 25 seconds. Sprinkle 2 tablespoons feta and half of spinach mixture across center of omelet.

4. Off heat, use spatula to fold lower third (portion nearest you) of omelet over filling; press gently with spatula to secure seam, maintaining fold. Run spatula between outer edge of omelet and skillet to loosen. Pull skillet sharply toward you few times to slide unfolded edge of omelet up far side of skillet. Jerk skillet again so that unfolded edge folds over itself, or use spatula to fold edge over. Invert omelet onto plate. Tidy edges with spatula and serve immediately.

5. Wipe skillet clean with paper towels and repeat with remaining 1 teaspoon oil, remaining eggs, remaining 2 tablespoons feta, and remaining filling.

Nutrition Info: 270 cal., 20g fat (6g sag. fat), 385mg chol, 320mg sod., 6g carb (2g sugars, 2g fiber), 16g pro.

Busy Day Breakfast Burrito

Servings: 4
Cooking Time: 3 Minutes

Ingredients:
- 1 1/2 cups egg substitute
- 4 (6-inch) whole-wheat flour tortillas
- 1/4 cup fresh, no-salt-added pico de gallo
- 1/2 cup shredded, reduced-fat, sharp cheddar cheese

Directions:

1. Place a small nonstick skillet over medium heat until hot. Coat the skillet with nonstick cooking spray, add egg substitute, and cook, without stirring, until egg mixture begins to set on bottom, about 1 minute.

2. Draw a spatula across the bottom of pan to form large curds. Continue cooking until egg mixture is thick but still moist; do not stir constantly.

3. Place the tortillas on a microwave-safe plate and microwave on HIGH for 15 seconds or until heated. Top each with equal amounts of the egg mixture.

4. Spoon 1 tablespoon pico de gallo evenly over the egg on each tortilla, sprinkle with 2 tablespoons cheese, and roll up.

Nutrition Info: 180 cal., 4g fat (2g sag. fat), 5mg chol, 450mg sod., 18g carb (2g sugars, 1g fiber), 16g pro.

BREAKFAST RECIPES

Kale Chips

Servings: 8

Cooking Time: 60 Minutes

Ingredients:
- 12 ounces Lacinato kale, stemmed and torn into 3-inch pieces
- 1 tablespoon extra-virgin olive oil
- ½ teaspoon kosher salt

Directions:

1. Adjust oven racks to upper-middle and lower-middle positions and heat oven to 200 degrees. Set wire racks in 2 rimmed baking sheets. Dry kale thoroughly between dish towels, transfer to large bowl, and toss with oil and salt.

2. Arrange kale on prepared racks, making sure leaves overlap as little as possible. Bake kale until very crisp, 45 to 60 minutes, switching and rotating sheets halfway through baking. Let kale chips cool completely before serving. (Kale chips can be stored in paper towel–lined airtight container for up to 1 day.)

Nutrition Info: 60 cal., 4g fat (0g sag. fat), 0mg chol, 160mg sod., 5g carb (1g sugars, 2g fiber), 3g pro.

BREAKFAST RECIPES

Cheesy Mushroom Omelet

Servings: 2
Cooking Time: 6 Minutes

Ingredients:
- 6 ounces sliced mushrooms
- 1/8 teaspoon black pepper
- 1/3 cup finely chopped green onion (green and white parts)
- 1 cup egg substitute
- 2 tablespoons crumbled bleu cheese (about 1/4 cup) or 1/4 cup shredded, reduced-fat, sharp cheddar cheese

Directions:
1. Place a small skillet over medium-high heat until hot. Coat with nonstick cooking spray and add mushrooms and pepper. Coat the mushrooms with nonstick cooking spray and cook 4 minutes or until soft, stirring frequently.
2. Add the onions and cook 1 minute longer. Set the pan aside.
3. Place another small skillet over medium heat until hot. Coat with nonstick cooking spray and add the egg substitute. Cook 1 minute without stirring. Using a rubber spatula, lift up the edges to allow the uncooked portion to run under. Cook 1–2 minutes longer or until eggs are almost set and beginning to puff up slightly.
4. Spoon the mushroom mixture on one half of the omelet, sprinkle the cheese evenly over the mushrooms, and gently fold over. Cut in half to serve.

Nutrition Info: 110 cal., 2g fat (1g sag. fat), 5mg chol, 340mg sod., 6g carb (3g sugars, 1g fiber), 16g pro.

BREAKFAST RECIPES

Double-Duty Banana Pancakes

Servings: 8

Cooking Time: 6 Minutes

Ingredients:
- 2 ripe medium bananas, thinly sliced
- 1 cup buckwheat pancake mix
- 3/4 cup plus 2 tablespoons fat-free milk
- 4 tablespoons light pancake syrup

Directions:

1. Mash one half of the banana slices and place in a medium bowl with the pancake mix and the milk. Stir until just blended.

2. Place a large nonstick skillet over medium heat until hot. (To test, sprinkle with a few drops of water. If the water drops "dance" or jump in the pan, it's hot enough.) Coat the skillet with nonstick cooking spray, add two scant 1/4 cup measures of batter, and cook the pancakes until puffed and dry around the edges, about 1 minute.

3. Flip the pancakes and cook until golden on the bottom. Place on a plate and cover to keep warm.

4. Recoat the skillet with nonstick cooking spray, add three scant 1/4 cup measures of batter, and cook as directed. Repeat with the remaining batter.

5. Place 2 pancakes on each of 4 dinner plates, top with equal amounts of banana slices, and drizzle evenly with the syrup. If you like, place the dinner plates in a warm oven and add the pancakes as they are cooked.

Nutrition Info: 100 cal., 0g fat (0g sag. fat), 0mg chol, 140mg sod., 23g carb (9g sugars, 2g fiber), 3g pro.

DIABETES COOKBOOK

Raisin French Toast With Apricot Spread

Servings: 4

Cooking Time: 6 Minutes Per Batch

Ingredients:

- 8 slices whole-wheat cinnamon raisin bread
- 3 tablespoons no-trans-fat margarine (35% vegetable oil)
- 1/4 cup apricot or any flavor all-fruit spread
- 1 cup egg substitute (divided use)

Directions:

1. Arrange 4 bread slices on the bottom of a 13 × 9-inch baking pan. Pour 1/2 cup egg substitute evenly over all and turn several times to coat. Let stand 2 minutes to absorb egg slightly.
2. Meanwhile, using a fork, stir the margarine and fruit spread together in a small bowl until well blended.
3. Place a large nonstick skillet over medium heat until hot. Liberally coat the skillet with nonstick cooking spray, add 4 bread slices (leaving any remaining egg mixture in the baking pan), and cook 3 minutes.
4. Turn and cook 3 minutes longer or until the bread is golden brown. For darker toast, turn the slices again and cook 1 minute more. Set aside on a serving platter and cover to keep warm.
5. While the first batch is cooking, place the remaining bread slices in the baking pan and pour the remaining egg substitute evenly over all. Turn several times to coat. Cook as directed.
6. Serve each piece of toast topped with 1 tablespoon of the margarine mixture.

Nutrition Info: 260 cal., 6g fat (1g sag. fat), 0mg chol, 390mg sod., 37g carb (17g sugars, 4g fiber), 12g pro.

Strawberry-Carrot Smoothies

Servings: 5

Cooking Time: 5 Minutes

Ingredients:
- 2 cups (16 ounces) reduced-fat plain Greek yogurt
- 1 cup carrot juice
- 1 cup orange juice
- 1 cup frozen pineapple chunks
- 1 cup frozen unsweetened sliced strawberries

Directions:

1. Place all ingredients in a blender; cover and process until smooth.

Nutrition Info: 141 cal., 2g fat (1g sat. fat), 5mg chol., 79mg sod., 20g carb. (15g sugars, 1g fiber), 10g pro.

Breakfast Grilled Swiss Cheese And Rye

Servings: 2

Cooking Time: 7 Minutes

Ingredients:

- 2 slices rye bread
- 4 teaspoons reduced-fat margarine (35% vegetable oil)
- 2 large eggs
- 1 1/2 ounces sliced, reduced-fat Swiss cheese, torn in small pieces

Directions:

1. Spread one side of each bread slice with 1 teaspoon margarine and set aside.
2. Place a medium skillet over medium heat until hot. Coat with nonstick cooking spray and add the egg substitute. Cook 1 minute without stirring. Using a rubber spatula, lift up the edges to allow the uncooked portion to run under. Cook 1–2 minutes longer or until eggs are almost set and beginning to puff up slightly. Flip and cook 30 seconds.
3. Remove the skillet from the heat and spoon half of the eggs on the unbuttered sides of two of the bread slices. Arrange equal amounts of the cheese evenly over each piece.
4. Return the skillet to medium heat until hot. Coat the skillet with nonstick cooking spray. Add the two sandwiches and cook 3 minutes. If the cheese doesn't melt when frying the sandwich bottom, put it under the broiler until brown. Using a serrated knife, cut each sandwich in half.

Nutrition Info: 250 cal., 13g fat (4g sag. fat), 200mg chol, 360mg sod., 17g carb (2g sugars, 2g fiber), 16g pro.

BREAKFAST RECIPES

English Muffin Melts

Servings: 8

Cooking Time: 3 Minutes

Ingredients:
- 4 whole-wheat English muffins, cut in half
- 2 tablespoons reduced-fat mayonnaise
- 3 ounces sliced reduced-fat Swiss cheese, torn in small pieces
- 4 ounces oven-roasted deli turkey, finely chopped

Directions:

1. Preheat the broiler.

2. Arrange the muffin halves on a baking sheet and place under the broiler for 1–2 minutes or until lightly toasted. Remove from broiler and spread 3/4 teaspoon mayonnaise over each muffin half.

3. Arrange the cheese pieces evenly on each muffin half and top with the turkey.

4. Return to the broiler and cook 3 minutes, or until the turkey is just beginning to turn golden and the cheese has melted.

Nutrition Info: 120 cal., 3g fat (1g sag. fat), 15mg chol, 290mg sod., 15g carb (3g sugars, 2g fiber), 9g pro.

BREAKFAST RECIPES

Peach Cranberry Quick Bread

Servings: 14

Cooking Time: 45 Minutes

Ingredients:
- 1 (15.6-ounce) box cranberry quick bread and muffin mix
- 1 cup water
- 1/2 cup egg substitute or 4 large egg whites
- 2 tablespoons canola oil
- 2 cups chopped frozen and thawed unsweetened peaches

Directions:
1. Preheat the oven to 375°F.
2. Coat a nonstick 9 × 5-inch loaf pan with nonstick cooking spray.
3. Beat the bread mix, water, egg substitute, and oil in a medium bowl for 50 strokes or until well blended. Stir in the peaches and spoon into the loaf pan. Bake 45 minutes or until a wooden toothpick comes out clean.
4. Place the loaf pan on a wire rack for 20 minutes before removing the bread from the pan. Cool completely for peak flavor and texture.

Nutrition Info: 150 cal., 3g fat (0g sag. fat), 0mg chol, 150mg sod., 29g carb (15g sugars, 1g fiber), 3g pro.

Orange-Honey Yogurt

Servings: 1

Cooking Time: 7 Minutes

Ingredients:

- 1 cup 2 percent Greek yogurt
- 2 tablespoons honey
- ¼ teaspoon grated orange zest plus 2 tablespoons juice

Directions:

1. Whisk ingredients together in bowl. (Yogurt can be refrigerated for up to 3 days.) Serve.

Nutrition Info: 15 cal., 0g fat (0g sag. fat), 0mg chol, 0mg sod., 2g carb (2g sugars, 0g fiber), 1g pro.

VEGETARIAN RECIPES

Black Bean And Corn Bowl

Servings: 4

Cooking Time: 22 Minutes

Ingredients:
- 1 (10.5-ounce) can mild tomatoes with green chilis
- 1 (15-ounce) can black beans, rinsed and drained
- 2 cups frozen corn kernels
- 1/4 cup reduced-fat sour cream

Directions:

1. Place all ingredients except the sour cream in a large saucepan. Bring to a boil over high heat, then reduce the heat, cover, and simmer 20 minutes.

2. Serve in 4 individual bowls topped with 1 tablespoon sour cream.

Nutrition Info: 170 cal., 2g fat (1g sag. fat), 5mg chol, 310mg sod., 31g carb (6g sugars, 7g fiber), 9g pro.

VEGETARIAN RECIPES

Cauliflower Steaks With Chimichurri Sauce

Servings: 4

Cooking Time: 10 Minutes

Ingredients:
- 2 heads cauliflower (2 pounds each)
- ¼ cup extra-virgin olive oil
- Salt and pepper
- 1 recipe Chimichurri (this page)
- Lemon wedges

Directions:

1. Adjust oven rack to lowest position and heat oven to 500 degrees. Working with 1 head cauliflower at a time, discard outer leaves and trim stem flush with bottom florets. Halve cauliflower lengthwise through core. Cut one 1½-inch-thick slab lengthwise from each half, trimming any florets not connected to core. Repeat with remaining cauliflower. (You should have 4 steaks; reserve remaining cauliflower for another use.)

2. Place steaks on rimmed baking sheet and drizzle with 2 tablespoons oil. Sprinkle with pinch salt and ⅛ teaspoon pepper and rub to distribute. Flip steaks and repeat.

3. Cover sheet tightly with foil and roast for 5 minutes. Remove foil and continue to roast until bottoms of steaks are well browned, 8 to 10 minutes. Gently flip and continue to roast until cauliflower is tender and second sides are well browned, 6 to 8 minutes.

4. Transfer steaks to serving platter and brush tops evenly with ¼ cup chimichurri. Serve with lemon wedges and remaining chimichurri.

Nutrition Info: 370 cal., 29g fat (4g sag. fat), 0mg chol, 300mg sod., 24g carb (9g sugars, 10g fiber), 9g pro.

VEGETARIAN RECIPES

"Refried" Bean And Rice Casserole

Servings: 4

Cooking Time: 15 Minutes

Ingredients:
- 2 1/4 cups cooked brown rice (omit added salt or fat)
- 1 (15.5-ounce) can dark red kidney beans, rinsed and drained
- 7 tablespoons picante sauce
- 1/4 cup water
- 1/2 cup shredded, reduced-fat, sharp cheddar cheese

Directions:

1. Preheat the oven to 350°F.
2. Coat an 8-inch-square baking pan with nonstick cooking spray. Place the rice in the pan and set aside.
3. Add the beans, picante sauce, and water to a blender and blend until pureed, scraping the sides of the blender frequently.
4. Spread the bean mixture evenly over the rice and sprinkle with cheese. Bake, uncovered, for 15 minutes or until thoroughly heated.

Nutrition Info: 260 cal., 3g fat (1g sag. fat), 5mg chol, 430mg sod., 44g carb (1g sugars, 7g fiber), 14g pro.

Pesto Potatoes And Edamame Bake

Servings: 4

Cooking Time: 1 Hour

Ingredients:
- 1 1/2 pounds red potatoes, cut into 1/4-inch-thick slices
- 1 cup fresh or frozen, thawed shelled edamame
- 1/2 cup prepared basil pesto
- 1/4 cup salted hulled pumpkin seeds

Directions:

1. Preheat oven to 350°F.

2. Coat a 2-quart baking dish with cooking spray. Arrange half of the potatoes on bottom of baking dish, overlapping slightly. Spoon half of the pesto evenly over all, top with the edamame, sprinkle with 1/4 teaspoon pepper. Repeat with remaining potatoes and pesto.

3. Cover and bake 55 minutes or until tender. Sprinkle with pumpkin seeds and bake, uncovered, 5 minutes.

Nutrition Info: 370 cal., 22g fat (3g sag. fat), 5mg chol, 380mg sod., 33g carb (3g sugars, 2g fiber), 14g pro.

VEGETARIAN RECIPES

Hurried Hummus Wraps

Servings: 4

Cooking Time: 5 Minutes

Ingredients:
- 4 whole-wheat flour tortillas
- 1/2 cup prepared hummus
- 6 cups packed mixed greens or spring greens
- 2 ounces crumbled reduced-fat feta or reduced-fat bleu cheese

Directions:

1. Warm tortillas according to package directions.
2. Top each with 2 tablespoons hummus, 1 1/2 cups lettuce, and 2 tablespoons cheese, roll tightly and cut in half.

Nutrition Info: 210 cal., 14g fat (2g sag. fat), 5mg chol, 420mg sod., 28g carb (1g sugars, 4g fiber), 8g pro.

VEGETARIAN RECIPES

Speedy Greek Orzo Salad

Servings: 9

Cooking Time: 7 Minutes

Ingredients:
- 8 ounces uncooked whole-wheat orzo pasta
- 1/2 cup reduced-fat olive oil vinaigrette salad dressing (divided use)
- 3 tablespoons salt-free Greek seasoning (sold in jars in the spice aisle)
- 2 ounces crumbled, reduced-fat, sun-dried tomato and basil feta cheese
- 2 tablespoons chopped fresh parsley (optional)

Directions:
1. Cook the pasta according to package directions, omitting any salt and fat.
2. Meanwhile, stir 1/4 cup salad dressing and the Greek seasoning together in a medium bowl.
3. Drain the pasta in a colander and run under cold water until cooled. Shake off excess liquid and add it to the salad dressing mixture. Toss well, then add the feta and toss gently. Cover the bowl with plastic wrap and refrigerate at least 1 hour.
4. At serving time, add 1/4 cup salad dressing and toss to coat. Sprinkle with 2 tablespoons chopped fresh parsley, if desired.

Nutrition Info: 130 cal., 4g fat (1g sag. fat), 5mg chol, 180mg sod., 20g carb (1g sugars, 5g fiber), 4g pro.

VEGETARIAN RECIPES

Tomato Topper Over Anything

Servings: 3

Cooking Time: 22 Minutes

Ingredients:
- 1 (14.5-ounce) can no-salt-added tomatoes with green pepper and onion
- 1/2 cup chopped roasted red peppers
- 2–3 tablespoons chopped fresh basil
- 2 teaspoons extra virgin olive oil

Directions:

1. Bring the tomatoes and peppers to boil in a medium saucepan. Reduce the heat and simmer, uncovered, for 15 minutes or until slightly thickened, stirring occasionally.

2. Remove the mixture from the heat, stir in the basil and oil, and let stand 5 minutes to develop flavors.

Nutrition Info: 80 cal., 3g fat (0g sag. fat), 0mg chol, 90mg sod., 12g carb (8g sugars, 2g fiber), 2g pro.

DIABETES COOKBOOK

VEGETARIAN RECIPES

Skillet-Grilled Meatless Burgers With Spicy Sour Cream

Servings: 4

Cooking Time: 15 Minutes

Ingredients:

- 4 soy protein burgers (preferably the grilled variety)
- 1 1/2 cups thinly sliced onions
- 1/8 teaspoon salt (divided use)
- 1/4 cup fat-free sour cream
- 4–6 drops chipotle-flavored hot sauce

Directions:

1. Place a large nonstick skillet over medium heat until hot. Coat the skillet with nonstick cooking spray, add the patties, and cook 4 minutes on each side. Set the patties aside on a separate plate and cover with foil to keep warm.

2. Coat the skillet with nonstick cooking spray and increase the heat to medium high. Add the onions and 1/16 teaspoon salt. Lightly coat the onions with nonstick cooking spray and cook 5 minutes or until they are richly browned, stirring frequently.

3. Meanwhile, stir the sour cream, hot sauce, and 1/16 teaspoon salt together in a small bowl.

4. When the onions are browned, push them to one side of the skillet and add the patties. Spoon the onions on top of the patties and cook 1–2 minutes longer to heat thoroughly. Top each patty with 1 tablespoon sour cream.

Nutrition Info: 120 cal., 2g fat (0g sag. fat), 5mg chol, 440mg sod., 12g carb (2g sugars, 7g fiber), 16g pro.

Feta Basil Pasta

Servings: 4

Cooking Time: 15 Minutes

Ingredients:
- 6 ounces whole-grain spaghetti, broken in half
- 4 ounces crumbled reduced-fat feta cheese
- 1/2 cup chopped fresh basil
- 1 cup grape tomatoes, quartered

Directions:

1. Cook pasta according to package directions, and drain.
2. Place pasta in a shallow bowl or rimmed platter. Top with the remaining ingredients in the order listed and sprinkle with 1/8 teaspoon salt and 1/8 teaspoon pepper, if desired.

Nutrition Info: 200 cal., 2g fat (0g sag. fat), 5mg chol, 250mg sod., 34g carb (1g sugars, 1g fiber), 14g pro.

Toasted Grain And Arugula

Servings: 4

Cooking Time: 20 Minutes

Ingredients:
- 4 ounces slivered almonds
- 1 cup dry bulgur
- 4 cups arugula
- 1/2 cup lite balsamic salad dressing

Directions:

1. Heat a large skillet over medium-high heat. Add the almonds and cook 2 minutes or until beginning to lightly brown, stirring constantly. Set aside on separate plate.

2. Add the bulgur to the skillet and cook (in the dry skillet) 3 minutes or until beginning to lightly brown, stirring constantly. Add 2 cups water, bring to a boil, reduce heat to low, cover, and simmer 12 minutes or until liquid is absorbed.

3. Remove from heat, place in a bowl with the arugula, 1/8 teaspoon salt, and 1/8 teaspoon pepper, if desired. Toss until arugula is slightly wilted.

4. Add the dressing to the skillet. Bring to a boil over medium-high heat and cook 2 minutes or until reduced to 1/3 cup. Immediately pour over the bulgur mixture and toss until well blended.

Nutrition Info: 310 cal., 16g fat (1g sag. fat), 0mg chol, 380mg sod., 39g carb (3g sugars, 10g fiber), 11g pro.

Open-Faced Grilled Pepper-Goat Cheese Sandwiches

Servings: 4

Cooking Time: 25 Minutes

Ingredients:
- 3 large red bell peppers, halved lengthwise
- 1 1/2 tablespoons balsamic vinegar
- 8 ounces whole grain loaf bread, cut in half lengthwise
- 2 ounces crumbled goat cheese

Directions:

1. Heat grill or grill pan over medium-high heat. Flatten pepper halves with palm of hand. Coat both sides with cooking spray and cook 20 minutes or until tender, turning frequently. Place on cutting board and coarsely chop. Combine the peppers with the vinegar and 1/8 teaspoon salt, if desired. Cover to keep warm.

2. Coat both sides of the bread with cooking spray and cook 1 1/2 to 2 minutes on each side or until lightly browned. Cut each bread half crosswise into 4 pieces.

3. Top each bread slice with 1/4 cup pepper mixture and sprinkle cheese evenly over all.

Nutrition Info: 250 cal., 7g fat (3g sag. fat), 10mg chol, 280mg sod., 33g carb (10g sugars, 7g fiber), 12g pro.

VEGETARIAN RECIPES

Cheesy Tortilla Rounds

Servings: 4

Cooking Time: 14 Minutes

Ingredients:
- 4 (6-inch) soft corn tortillas
- 1 cup fat-free refried beans
- 1/2 cup shredded, reduced-fat mozzarella cheese
- 1 poblano chili pepper, seeded and thinly sliced, or 2 jalapeño chili peppers, seeded and thinly sliced

Directions:

1. Preheat the broiler.

2. Place a large nonstick skillet over medium-high heat until hot. Coat the skillet with nonstick cooking spray. Place two tortillas in the skillet and cook 1 minute or until they begin to lightly brown on the bottom. Turn them and cook 1 minute, then place on a baking sheet. Repeat with the other two tortillas.

3. Return the skillet to medium-high heat, coat with nonstick cooking spray, and add the peppers. Coat the peppers with nonstick cooking spray and cook 6 minutes or until they are tender and brown, stirring frequently. Remove them from the heat.

4. Spread equal amounts of beans evenly on each tortilla. Broil 4 inches away from the heat source for 1 minute. Sprinkle the cheese and pepper slices evenly over each tortilla and broil another 2 minutes or until the cheese has melted. Serve with lime wedges, if desired.

Nutrition Info: 150 cal., 3g fat (1g sag. fat), 10mg chol, 370mg sod., 23g carb (2g sugars, 5g fiber), 9g pro.

SALADS RECIPES

Zesty Citrus Melon

Servings: 4

Cooking Time: 5 Minutes

Ingredients:
- 1/4 cup orange juice
- 2–3 tablespoons lemon juice
- 1 teaspoon honey
- 3 cups diced honeydew or cantaloupe melon

Directions:

1. Stir the orange juice, lemon zest (if using), lemon juice, and honey together in a small bowl.
2. Place the melon on a serving plate and pour the juice mixture evenly over all. For peak flavor, serve within 1 hour.

Nutrition Info: 60 cal., 0g fat (0g sag. fat), 0mg chol, 25mg sod., 15g carb (13g sugars, 1g fiber), 1g pro.

Toasted Pecan And Apple Salad

Servings: 4

Cooking Time: 8 Minutes

Ingredients:
- 2 tablespoons pecan chips
- 2 cups chopped unpeeled red apples
- 1/4 cup dried raisin-cherry blend (or 1/4 cup dried cherries or golden raisins alone)
- 1 teaspoon honey (or 1 teaspoon packed dark brown sugar and 1 teaspoon water)

Directions:

SALADS RECIPES

1. Place a small skillet over medium-high heat until hot. Add the pecans and cook 1–2 minutes or until beginning to lightly brown, stirring constantly. Remove from the heat and set aside on paper towels to stop the cooking process and cool quickly.
2. Combine the apples and dried fruit in a medium bowl, drizzle honey over all, and toss gently.
3. Serve on a lettuce leaf (if desired) or a pretty salad plate. Sprinkle each serving evenly with the pecans.

Nutrition Info: 90 cal., 2g fat (0g sag. fat), 0mg chol, 0mg sod., 18g carb (14g sugars, 2g fiber), 1g pro.

Seaside Shrimp Salad

Servings: 4

Cooking Time: 5 Minutes

Ingredients:
- 1 1/2 pounds peeled raw fresh or frozen and thawed shrimp
- 2 tablespoons reduced-fat mayonnaise
- 1 1/2 teaspoons seafood seasoning
- 6 tablespoons lemon juice

Directions:
1. Bring water to boil in a large saucepan over high heat. Add the shrimp and return to a boil. Reduce the heat and simmer, uncovered, 2–3 minutes or until the shrimp is opaque in the center.
2. Drain the shrimp in a colander, rinse with cold water for 30 seconds, and pat dry with paper towels. Let stand 10 minutes to cool completely.
3. Place shrimp in a medium bowl with the mayonnaise, seafood seasoning, and lemon juice. Stir gently to coat. Cover with plastic wrap and refrigerate 2 hours. Serve as is or over tomato slices or lettuce leaves.

Nutrition Info: 130 cal., 2g fat (0g sag. fat), 205mg chol, 430mg sod., 3g carb (1g sugars, 0g fiber), 26g pro.

SALADS RECIPES

Caesar'd Chicken Salad

Servings: 4

Cooking Time: 5 Minutes

Ingredients:

- 1/4 cup fat-free mayonnaise
- 3 tablespoons fat-free Caesar salad dressing
- 2 1/2 cups cooked diced chicken breast
- 1/2 cup finely chopped green onion (green and white parts)

Directions:

1. Stir the mayonnaise and salad dressing together in a medium bowl. Add the chicken, onions, and black pepper, if desired, and stir until well coated.

2. Cover with plastic wrap and refrigerate at least 2 hours to allow flavors to blend. You may refrigerate this salad up to 24 hours before serving.

Nutrition Info: 170 cal., 3g fat (1g sag. fat), 75mg chol, 460mg sod., 4g carb (2g sugars, 1g fiber), 28g pro.

Tangy Sweet Carrot Pepper Salad

Servings: 4

Cooking Time: 1 Minute

Ingredients:

- 1 1/2 cups peeled sliced carrots (about 1/8-inch thick)
- 2 tablespoons water
- 3/4 cup thinly sliced green bell pepper
- 1/3 cup thinly sliced onion
- 1/4 cup reduced-fat Catalina dressing

Directions:

1. Place carrots and water in a shallow, microwave-safe dish, such as a glass pie plate. Cover with plastic wrap and microwave on HIGH for 1 minute or until carrots are just tender-crisp. Be careful not to overcook them—the carrots should retain some crispness.

2. Immediately place the carrots in a colander and run under cold water about 30 seconds to cool. Shake to drain and place the carrots on paper towels to dry further. Dry the dish.

3. When the carrots are completely cool, return them to the dish, add the remaining ingredients, and toss gently to coat.

4. Serve immediately, or chill 30 minutes for a more blended flavor. Flavors are at their peak if you serve this salad within 30 minutes of adding dressing.

Nutrition Info: 60 cal., 0g fat (0g sag. fat), 0mg chol, 200mg sod., 11g carb (7g sugars, 2g fiber), 1g pro.

Feta'd Tuna With Greens

Servings: 4

Cooking Time: 6 Minutes

Ingredients:
- 6 cups torn Boston Bibb lettuce, red leaf lettuce, or spring greens
- 3 tablespoons fat-free Caesar salad dressing
- 2 ounces crumbled, reduced-fat, sun-dried tomato and basil feta cheese
- 1 (6.4-ounce) packet tuna, broken in large chunks

Directions:

1. Place the lettuce and salad dressing in a large bowl and toss gently, yet thoroughly, to coat completely.

2. Place 1 1/2 cups of lettuce on each of 4 salad plates. Sprinkle each salad with 1 tablespoon feta and lightly flake equal amounts of tuna in the center of each serving. If desired, add a small amount of dressing (such as fat-free Caesar) to the lettuce.

Nutrition Info: 80 cal., 2g fat (1g sag. fat), 25mg chol, 360mg sod., 3g carb (1g sugars, 2g fiber), 15g pro.

SALADS RECIPES

Bibb Lettuce Salad With Endive And Cucumber

Servings: 4

Cooking Time: 12minutes

Ingredients:
- 12 ounces cherry tomatoes, halved
- 1 head Bibb lettuce (8 ounces), leaves separated and torn into bite-size pieces
- 1 head Belgian endive (4 ounces), cut into ½-inch pieces
- 1 cucumber, peeled, halved lengthwise, seeded, and sliced ¼ inch thick
- 1 recipe Parmesan-Peppercorn Dressing (this page)

Directions:

1. Gently toss lettuce and chickpeas with vinaigrette in bowl until well coated. Sprinkle with feta. Serve.

Nutrition Info: 110 cal., 7g fat (1g sag. fat), 5mg chol, 140mg sod., 8g carb (4g sugars, 3g fiber), 4g pro.

Creamy Dill Cucumbers

Servings: 4

Cooking Time: 6 Minutes

Ingredients:
- 1/4 cup plain fat-free yogurt
- 1 tablespoon reduced-fat mayonnaise
- 1/2 teaspoon dried dill
- 1/4 teaspoon salt
- 2 cups peeled diced cucumber

Directions:

1. Stir the yogurt, mayonnaise, dill, and salt together in a small bowl until completely blended.

2. Place the cucumbers in a medium bowl, add the yogurt mixture, and toss gently to coat completely.

DIABETES COOKBOOK

SALADS RECIPES

3. Serve within 30 minutes for peak flavors and texture.

Nutrition Info: 25 cal., 1g fat (0g sag. fat), 0mg chol, 190mg sod., 3g carb (2g sugars, 0g fiber), 1g pro.

Ginger'd Ambrosia

Servings: 4
Cooking Time: 5–10 Minutes

Ingredients:
- 3 medium navel oranges, peeled and cut into bite-sized sections (about 1 1/2 cups total)
- 3 tablespoons flaked, sweetened, shredded coconut
- 2–3 teaspoons grated gingerroot
- 4 fresh or canned pineapple slices, packed in juice, drained

Directions:
1. Place all ingredients except the pineapple in a medium bowl and toss gently. If desired, add 1 teaspoon pourable sugar substitute. Let stand 5–10 minutes to develop flavors.
2. Arrange each pineapple slice on a salad plate and spoon a rounded 1/3 cup of the orange mixture on each slice.

Nutrition Info: 80 cal., 1g fat (1g sag. fat), 0mg chol, 10mg sod., 18g carb (14g sugars, 3g fiber), 1g pro.

Orange Pomegranate Salad With Honey

Servings: 6
Cooking Time: 15 Minutes

Ingredients:
- 5 medium oranges or 10 clementines
- 1/2 cup pomegranate seeds
- 2 tablespoons honey

- 1 to 2 teaspoons orange flower water or orange juice

Directions:

1. Cut a thin slice from the top and bottom of each orange; stand orange upright on a cutting board. With a knife, cut off peel and outer membrane from oranges. Cut crosswise into 1/2-in. slices.

2. Arrange orange slices on a serving platter; sprinkle with pomegranate seeds. In a small bowl, mix honey and orange flower water; drizzle over fruit.

Nutrition Info: 62 cal., 0 fat (0 sat. fat), 0 chol., 2mg sod., 15g carb. (14g sugars, 0 fiber), 1g pro.

Minted Carrot Salad

Servings: 4

Cooking Time: 1 Minute

Ingredients:
- 3 cups thinly sliced carrots (about 12 ounces total)
- 1 tablespoon extra-virgin olive oil
- 1 tablespoon cider vinegar
- 1/3 cup chopped fresh mint (or basil)

Directions:

1. Bring 4 cups water to a rolling boil in a large saucepan. Add the carrots, return to a rolling boil, and cook 30 seconds. Immediately drain in a colander and run under cold water to cool completely. Drain well.

2. Place carrots in a shallow bowl. Top with remaining ingredients and sprinkle evenly with 1/4 teaspoon salt and 1/4 teaspoon pepper. Serve immediately or cover and refrigerate up to 1 hour before serving.

Nutrition Info: 75 cal., 4g fat (0g sag. fat), 0mg chol, 70mg sod., 10g carb (5g sugars, 4g fiber), 1g pro.

Mesclun Salad With Goat Cheese And Almonds

Servings: 4

Cooking Time: 8 minutes

Ingredients:

- 5 ounces (5 cups) mesclun
- 3 tablespoons toasted sliced almonds
- 1 recipe Classic Vinaigrette (this page)
- 2 ounces goat cheese, crumbled (½ cup)

Directions:

1. Gently toss mesclun with almonds and vinaigrette in bowl until well coated. Sprinkle with goat cheese. Serve.

Nutrition Info: 170 cal., 16g fat (4g sag. fat), 5mg chol, 160mg sod., 1g carb (0g sugars, 1g fiber), 4g pro.

Carrot Cranberry Matchstick Salad

Servings: 4

Cooking Time: 5 Minutes

Ingredients:

- 3 cups matchstick carrots
- 1 poblano chili pepper, chopped
- 1/3 cup dried cranberries
- Zest and juice of 1 medium lemon

Directions:

1. Combine the ingredients with 1/8 teaspoon salt in a large bowl. Cover and refrigerate 1 hour before serving.

Nutrition Info: 70 cal., 0g fat (0g sag. fat), 0mg chol, 105mg sod., 19g carb (11g sugars, 4g fiber), 1g pro.

SALADS RECIPES

Crispy Crunch Coleslaw

Servings: 4

Cooking Time: 7 Minutes

Ingredients:
- 3 cups shredded cabbage mix with carrots and red cabbage
- 1 medium green bell pepper, finely chopped
- 2–3 tablespoons apple cider vinegar
- 2 tablespoons Splenda
- 1/8 teaspoon salt

Directions:

1. Place all ingredients in a large zippered plastic bag, seal tightly, and shake to blend thoroughly.

2. Refrigerate 3 hours before serving to blend flavors. This salad tastes best served the same day you make it.

Nutrition Info: 20 cal., 0g fat (0g sag. fat), 0mg chol, 85mg sod., 4g carb (2g sugars, 2g fiber), 0g pro.

MEAT RECIPES

Sweet Jerk Pork

Servings: 4

Cooking Time: 20 Minutes

Ingredients:
- 1 pound pork tenderloin
- 2 teaspoons jerk seasoning
- 2 tablespoons packed dark brown sugar
- 2 teaspoons Worcestershire sauce

Directions:

1. Preheat the oven to 425°F.
2. Sprinkle the pork evenly with the jerk seasoning and press down gently so the spices adhere. Let the pork stand 15 minutes.
3. Stir the sugar and Worcestershire sauce together in a small bowl until well blended. Coat an 11 x 7-inch baking pan with nonstick cooking spray and set aside.
4. Place a large nonstick skillet over medium-high heat until hot. Coat the skillet with nonstick cooking spray, add the pork, and brown all sides, about 5 minutes, turning occasionally.
5. Place the pork in the baking pan and spoon all but 1 tablespoon of the Worcestershire mixture evenly over the pork. Bake for 13–15 minutes or until the pork is barely pink in the center and a meat thermometer reaches 170°F.
6. Place the pork on a cutting board, spoon the remaining 1 tablespoon Worcestershire mixture evenly over all, and let stand 10 minutes before slicing.

Nutrition Info: 150 cal., 3g fat (1g sag. fat), 60mg chol, 210mg sod., 8g carb (8g sugars, 0g fiber), 22g pro.

MEAT RECIPES

Country-Style Ham And Potato Casserole

Servings: 4

Cooking Time: 15 Minutes

Ingredients:
- 6 ounces lean smoked deli ham, (preferably Virginia ham), thinly sliced and chopped
- 1 pound red potatoes, scrubbed and thinly sliced
- 1 medium onion, thinly sliced
- 1/3 cup shredded, reduced-fat, sharp cheddar cheese

Directions:
1. Preheat the oven to 350°F.
2. Place a medium nonstick skillet over medium-high heat until hot. Coat the skillet with nonstick cooking spray, add ham, and cook 5 minutes or until the ham edges are beginning to lightly brown, stirring frequently. Remove from the heat and set the ham aside on a separate plate.
3. Layer half of the potatoes and half of the onions in the bottom of the skillet. Top with the ham and repeat with layers of potatoes and onions. Sprinkle with black pepper, if desired, and cover tightly with a sheet of foil.
4. Bake 35–40 minutes or until the potatoes are tender when pierced with a fork. Remove from the oven, top with cheese, and let stand, uncovered, for 3 minutes to melt the cheese and develop flavors.

Nutrition Info: 170 cal., 2g fat (1g sag. fat), 25mg chol, 420mg sod., 23g carb (4g sugars, 2g fiber), 13g pro.

MEAT RECIPES

Grapefruit-Zested Pork

Servings: 4
Cooking Time: 6 Minutes

Ingredients:
- 3 tablespoons lite soy sauce
- 1/2–1 teaspoon grapefruit zest
- 3 tablespoons grapefruit juice
- 1 jalapeño pepper, seeded and finely chopped, or 1/8–1/4 teaspoon dried red pepper flakes
- 4 thin lean pork chops with bone in (about 1 1/4 pounds total)

Directions:
1. Combine all ingredients in a large zippered plastic bag. Seal tightly and toss back and forth to coat evenly. Refrigerate overnight or at least 8 hours.
2. Preheat the broiler.
3. Coat the broiler rack and pan with nonstick cooking spray, arrange the pork chops on the rack (discarding the marinade), and broil 2 inches away from the heat source for 3 minutes. Turn and broil 3 minutes longer or until the pork is no longer pink in the center.

Nutrition Info: 130 cal., 3g fat (1g sag. fat), 60mg chol, 270mg sod., 2g carb (1g sugars, 0g fiber), 23g pro.

Zesty Beef Patties With Grilled Onions

Servings: 4

Cooking Time: 15 Minutes

Ingredients:
- 1 pound 96% lean ground beef
- 1 tablespoon Dijon mustard
- 4 teaspoons ranch-style salad dressing and seasoning mix (available in packets)
- 1 large yellow onion, thinly sliced
- 1/4 cup water

Directions:

1. Mix the ground beef, mustard, and salad dressing mix together in a medium bowl. Shape the beef mixture into 4 patties.

2. Place a large nonstick skillet over medium-high heat until hot. Coat the skillet with nonstick cooking spray and add the onions. Coat the onions with nonstick cooking spray and cook 7 minutes or until they are richly browned, stirring frequently. Set them aside on a separate plate.

3. Recoat the skillet with nonstick cooking spray, add the patties, and cook 4 minutes. Flip the patties and cook another 3 minutes or until they are no longer pink in the center. Place them on a serving platter.

4. Add the onions and water to the pan drippings and cook 30 seconds, scraping the bottom and sides of the skillet. When the mixture has thickened slightly, spoon it over the patties.

Nutrition Info: 190 cal., 5g fat (2g sag. fat), 65mg chol, 450mg sod., 8g carb (3g sugars, 1g fiber), 26g pro.

Pork With Tomato Caper Sauce

Servings: 4

Cooking Time: 10 Minutes

Ingredients:

- 2 tablespoons tomato paste with oregano, basil, and garlic
- 2 tablespoons capers, drained and mashed with a fork
- 2/3 cup water, divided use
- 1/8 teaspoon salt
- 4 (4-ounce) boneless pork chops, trimmed of fat

Directions:

1. Using a fork, stir the tomato paste, capers, and 1/3 cup water together in a small bowl.
2. Place a medium nonstick skillet over medium-high heat until hot. Coat the skillet with nonstick cooking spray, add the pork chops, and cook 3 minutes.
3. Turn the pork chops and immediately reduce the heat to medium. Spoon the tomato mixture evenly on top of each pork chop, cover tightly, and cook 5 minutes or until the pork chops are barely pink in the center. The sauce may be dark in some areas.
4. Remove the skillet from the heat and add the remaining 1/3 cup water and salt. Turn the pork chops over several times to remove the sauce. Place the pork chops on a serving plate and set aside.
5. Increase the heat to medium high. Bring the sauce to a boil, stirring constantly, and boil 1 minute or until the sauce begins to thicken slightly and measures 1/2 cup. Spoon the sauce over the pork chops.

Nutrition Info: 140 cal., 3g fat (1g sag. fat), 65mg chol, 330mg sod., 2g carb (1g sugars, 0g fiber), 25g pro.

Homestyle Double-Onion Roast

Servings: 6

Cooking Time: 1 Hour And 10 Minutes

Ingredients:
- 1 pound carrots, scrubbed, quartered lengthwise, and cut into 3-inch pieces
- 2 medium onions (8 ounces total), cut in 1/2-inch wedges and separated
- 1 3/4 pounds lean eye of round roast
- 1/4 cup water
- 2 1/2 tablespoons onion soup mix

Directions:

1. Preheat the oven to 325°F.
2. Coat a 13 x 9-inch nonstick baking pan with nonstick cooking spray, arrange the carrots and onions in the pan, and set aside.
3. Place a medium nonstick skillet over medium-high heat until hot. Coat the skillet with nonstick cooking spray, add the beef, and brown 2 minutes. Turn and brown another 2 minutes.
4. Place the beef in the center of the baking pan on top of the vegetables. Add the water to the skillet and scrap up the pan drippings, then pour them over the beef. Sprinkle evenly with the soup mix.
5. Cover the pan tightly with foil and cook 1 hour and 5 minutes or until a meat thermometer reaches 135°F. Place the beef on a cutting board and let stand 15 minutes before slicing. (The temperature will rise another 10°F while the beef stands.)
6. Keep the vegetables in the pan covered to keep warm. Place the beef slices on a serving platter, arrange the vegetables around the beef, and spoon the pan liquids evenly over the beef.

Nutrition Info: 220 cal., 4g fat (1g sag. fat), 60mg chol, 410mg sod., 13g carb (5g sugars, 3g fiber), 32g pro.

MEAT RECIPES

Grilled Dijon Pork Roast

Servings: 12
Cooking Time: 1 Hour

Ingredients:
- 1/3 cup balsamic vinegar
- 3 tablespoons Dijon mustard
- 1 tablespoon honey
- 1 teaspoon salt
- 1 boneless pork loin roast (3 to 4 pounds)

Directions:

1. In a large resealable plastic bag, whisk vinegar, mustard, honey and salt. Add pork; seal the bag and turn to coat. Refrigerate for at least 8 hours or overnight.
2. Prepare grill for indirect heat, using a drip pan.
3. Drain pork, discarding marinade. Place pork on a greased grill rack over drip pan and cook, covered, over indirect medium heat for 1 to 1 1/2 hours or until a thermometer reads 145°, turning occasionally. Let stand for 10 minutes before slicing.

Nutrition Info: 149 cal., 5g fat (2g sat. fat), 56mg chol., 213mg sod., 2g carb. (1g sugars, 0 fiber), 22g pro.

Spicy Chili'd Sirloin Steak

Servings: 4
Cooking Time: 11 Minutes

Ingredients:
- 1 pound boneless sirloin steak, trimmed of fat
- 2 tablespoons chili seasoning (available in packets)
- 1/8 teaspoon salt

Directions:

MEAT RECIPES

1. Coat both sides of the sirloin with the chili seasoning mix, pressing down so the spices adhere. Let stand 15 minutes, or overnight in the refrigerator for a spicier flavor (let steak stand at room temperature 15 minutes before cooking).

2. Place a large nonstick skillet over medium-high heat until hot. Coat the skillet with nonstick cooking spray, add the beef, and cook 5 minutes. Turn the steak, reduce the heat to medium, cover tightly, and cook 5 minutes. Do not overcook. Remove the skillet from the heat and let stand 2 minutes, covered.

3. Sprinkle the steak with salt and cut into 1/4-inch slices. Pour any accumulated juices over the steak slices.

Nutrition Info: 140 cal., 4g fat (1g sag. fat), 40mg chol, 250mg sod., 2g carb (0g sugars, 0g fiber), 23g pro.

Sizzling Pork Chops

Servings: 4
Cooking Time: 12 Minutes

Ingredients:
- 4 (4-ounce) boneless pork chops, trimmed of fat
- 1 tablespoon dried zesty Italian salad dressing and recipe mix (available in packets)

Directions:

1. Coat both sides of the pork chops with the salad dressing mix, pressing down gently so the spices adhere.

2. Place a large nonstick skillet over medium heat until hot. Coat the skillet with nonstick cooking spray, add the pork, and cook 4 minutes. Turn and cook 4 minutes longer or until the pork is barely pink in the center.

3. Remove the skillet from the heat and let the pork stand in the skillet 2–3 minutes or until the pork begins to release some of its juices. Move the pork pieces around in the skillet several times to absorb the pan residue.

Nutrition Info: 140 cal., 3g fat (1g sag. fat), 65mg chol, 390mg sod., 1g carb (1g sugars, 0g fiber), 25g pro.

MEAT RECIPES

Sausage Pilaf Peppers

Servings: 4

Cooking Time: 40 Minutes

Ingredients:

- 4 medium green bell peppers
- 6 ounces reduced-fat pork breakfast sausage
- 3/4 cup uncooked instant brown rice
- 2/3 cup salsa, divided use

Directions:

1. Preheat the oven to 350°F.
2. Slice the tops off of each pepper and discard the seeds and membrane, leaving the peppers whole.
3. Coat a large nonstick skillet with nonstick cooking spray and place over medium-high heat until hot. Add the sausage and cook until it's no longer pink, breaking up large pieces while stirring.
4. Remove from the heat and add the rice and all but 1/4 cup salsa. Stir gently to blend.
5. Fill the peppers with equal amounts of the mixture and top each with 1 tablespoon salsa. Place the peppers in the skillet and cover tightly with foil. Bake 35 minutes or until the peppers are tender.

Nutrition Info: 260 cal., 8g fat (2g sag. fat), 20mg chol, 450mg sod., 37g carb (5g sugars, 5g fiber), 11g pro.

Chili-Stuffed Potatoes

Servings: 4

Cooking Time: 10 Minutes

Ingredients:

- 4 (8-ounce) baking potatoes, preferably Yukon Gold, scrubbed and pierced several times with a fork
- 12 ounces 90% lean ground beef

DIABETES COOKBOOK

- 3/4 cup water
- 1 (1.25-ounce) packet chili seasoning mix

Directions:

1. Microwave the potatoes on HIGH 10–11 minutes or until they are tender when pierced with a fork.

2. Meanwhile, place a large nonstick skillet over medium-high heat until hot. Coat the skillet with nonstick cooking spray, add the beef, and cook until the beef is no longer pink, stirring frequently.

3. Add the water and chili seasoning and stir. Cook 1–2 minutes or until thickened.

4. Split the potatoes almost in half and fluff with a fork. Spoon 1/2 cup chili onto each potato and top with sour cream or cheese (if desired).

Nutrition Info: 350 cal., 8g fat (2g sag. fat), 50mg chol, 410mg sod., 48g carb (3g sugars, 5g fiber), 21g pro.

Easy & Elegant Tenderloin Roast

Servings: 12
Cooking Time: 50 Minutes

Ingredients:

- 1 beef tenderloin (5 pounds)
- 2 tablespoons olive oil
- 4 garlic cloves, minced
- 2 teaspoons sea salt
- 1 1/2 teaspoons coarsely ground pepper

Directions:

1. Preheat oven to 425°. Place roast on a rack in a shallow roasting pan. In a small bowl, mix the oil, garlic, salt and pepper; rub over roast.

2. Roast 50-70 minutes or until meat reaches desired doneness (for medium-rare, a thermometer should read 145°; medium, 160°). Remove from oven; tent with foil. Let stand 15 minutes before slicing.

Nutrition Info: 294 cal., 13g fat (5g sat. fat), 82mg chol., 394mg sod., 1g carb. (0 sugars, 0 fiber), 40g pro.

MEAT RECIPES

Sriracha-Roasted Pork With Sweet Potatoes

Servings: 4

Cooking Time: 25 Minutes

Ingredients:
- 1 pound pork tenderloin
- 1 pound sweet potatoes, peeled and cut into 1-inch chunks (1/4 tsp salt and pepper)
- 2 tablespoons honey
- 1 tablespoon hot pepper sauce, such as sriracha

Directions:

1. Preheat oven to 425°F.
2. Heat a large skillet coated with cooking spray over medium-high heat. Add the pork and brown on all sides, about 5 minutes total.
3. Place potatoes in a 13 × 9-inch baking pan. Coat potatoes with cooking spray and toss until well coated. Place the pork in the center of the potatoes and sprinkle 1/4 teaspoon salt and 1/4 teaspoon pepper evenly over all.
4. In a small bowl, combine the honey and sriracha sauce; set aside.
5. Bake 10 minutes, stir potatoes, spoon sauce over pork, and continue baking 15 minutes or until internal temperature of the pork reaches 150°F.
6. Place the pork on a cutting board and let stand 3 minutes before slicing. Meanwhile, gently toss the potatoes in the pan with any pan drippings. Cover to keep warm. Serve with pork.

Nutrition Info: 280 cal., 5g fat (1g sag. fat), 75mg chol, 310mg sod., 31g carb (6g sugars, 6g fiber), 26g pro.

Beef Strips With Sweet Ginger Sauce

Servings: 4

Cooking Time: 4 Minutes

Ingredients:
- 2 tablespoons lite soy sauce
- 1 tablespoon sugar
- 2 teaspoons grated gingerroot
- 1 pound boneless top round or sirloin steak, trimmed of fat and sliced into strips

Directions:

1. Stir the soy sauce, sugar, and gingerroot together in a small bowl and set aside.
2. Place a large nonstick skillet over medium-high heat until hot. Coat the skillet with nonstick cooking spray, add half the beef, and cook 1 minute, stirring constantly.
3. Remove the beef from the skillet and set aside on a separate plate. Recoat the skillet with nonstick cooking spray and cook the remaining beef 1 minute.
4. Return the first batch of beef to the skillet, add the soy sauce mixture, and cook 1 minute to heat thoroughly.

Nutrition Info: 150 cal., 3g fat (1g sag. fat), 60mg chol, 300mg sod., 4g carb (3g sugars, 0g fiber), 24g pro.

POULTRY RECIPES

Taco Chicken Tenders

Servings: 4

Cooking Time: 7 Minutes

Ingredients:

- 4 teaspoons taco seasoning mix (available in packets)
- 1 pound chicken tenderloins, rinsed and patted dry
- 1/2 medium lime
- 2 tablespoons fat-free sour cream

Directions:

1. Sprinkle the taco seasoning evenly over both sides of the chicken pieces, pressing down gently so the spices adhere.

2. Place a large nonstick skillet over medium-high heat until hot. Coat the skillet with nonstick cooking spray, add the chicken, and cook 2 minutes.

3. Turn gently to keep the seasonings on the chicken as much as possible, reduce the heat to medium, and cook 2 minutes. Turn gently and cook 2 more minutes or until the chicken is no longer pink in the center.

4. Remove from the heat, squeeze lime juice evenly over all, and serve with 1/2 tablespoon sour cream per serving.

Nutrition Info: 140 cal., 3g fat (0g sag. fat), 65mg chol, 290mg sod., 3g carb (1g sugars, 1g fiber), 24g pro.

Chicken Apple Sausage And Onion Smothered Grits

Servings: 4

Cooking Time: 10 Minutes

Ingredients:

- 2/3 cup dry quick cooking grits
- 8 ounces sliced fresh mushrooms
- 3 (4 ounces each) links fully cooked chicken apple sausage, thinly sliced, such as Al Fresco

- 1 1/2 cups chopped onion

Directions:

1. Bring 2 2/3 cups water to a boil in a medium saucepan. Slowly stir in the grits, reduce heat to medium-low, cover, and cook 5–7 minutes or until thickened.

2. Meanwhile, heat a large skillet coated with cooking spray over medium-high heat. Add the mushrooms and cook 4 minutes or until beginning to lightly brown. Set aside on separate plate.

3. Coat skillet with cooking spray and cook sausage 3 minutes or until browned on edges, stirring occasionally. Set aside with mushrooms. To pan residue, add onions, coat with cooking spray, and cook 4 minutes or until richly browned. Add the sausage and mushrooms back to the skillet with any accumulated juices and 1/4 cup water. Cook 1 minute to heat through.

4. Sprinkle with 1/8 teaspoon salt and 1/8 teaspoon pepper. Spoon equal amounts of the grits in each of 4 shallow soup bowls, top with the sausage mixture.

Nutrition Info: 270 cal., 7g fat (1g sag. fat), 60mg chol, 430mg sod., 31g carb (4g sugars, 3g fiber), 19g pro.

Hoisin Chicken

Servings: 4	Cooking Time: 8 Minutes

Ingredients:

- 3 tablespoons hoisin sauce
- 1 teaspoon orange zest
- 3 tablespoons orange juice
- 1 pound boneless, skinless chicken breasts, rinsed, patted dry, and cut into thin slices or strips

Directions:

1. Stir the hoisin sauce, orange zest, and juice together in a small bowl and set aside.

2. Place a medium nonstick skillet over medium-high heat until hot. Coat the skillet with nonstick cooking spray, add the chicken, and cook 6–7 minutes or until the chicken just begins to lightly brown. Use two utensils to stir as you would when stir-frying.

3. Place the chicken on a serving platter. Add the hoisin mixture to the skillet and cook 15 seconds, stirring constantly. Spoon evenly over the chicken.

Nutrition Info: 160 cal., 3g fat (0g sag. fat), 65mg chol, 260mg sod., 7g carb (4g sugars, 0g fiber), 24g pro.

Greek Chicken With Lemon

Servings: 4

Cooking Time: 50 Minutes

Ingredients:

- 8 chicken drumsticks, skin removed, rinsed and patted dry
- 2 tablespoons dried salt-free Greek seasoning (sold in jars in the spice aisle)
- 2 teaspoons extra virgin olive oil
- 1 teaspoon lemon zest
- 4 tablespoons lemon juice (divided use)

Directions:

1. Place the drumsticks, Greek seasoning, olive oil, lemon zest, and 2 tablespoons lemon juice in a gallon-sized zippered plastic bag. Seal the bag and toss back and forth to coat the chicken evenly. Refrigerate for 8 hours or up to 48 hours, turning occasionally.

2. Preheat the oven to 350°F.

3. Coat a 12 × 8-inch baking dish with nonstick cooking spray, arrange the drumsticks in a single layer, and pour the marinade evenly over all. Bake uncovered for 50–55 minutes or until the drumsticks are no longer pink in the center, turning occasionally.

4. Place the drumsticks on a serving platter. Add salt to taste, if desired, and 2 tablespoons lemon juice to a small bowl, stir to blend well, and pour evenly over the chicken pieces. Season with 1/8 teaspoon salt, if desired.

Nutrition Info: 210 cal., 8g fat (1g sag. fat), 95mg chol, 100mg sod., 2g carb (0g sugars, 1g fiber), 30g pro.

Sausage And Farro Mushrooms

Servings: 4
Cooking Time: 20 Minutes

Ingredients:
- 1/2 cup dry pearled farro
- 2 (3.9 ounces each) Italian turkey sausage links, removed from casing, such as Jennie-o
- 8 portabella mushroom caps, stems removed, caps wiped with damp cloth
- 2 tablespoons crumbled reduced-fat blue cheese

Directions:
1. Preheat broiler. Coat both sides of the mushrooms with cooking spray, place on a foil-lined baking sheet, and broil 5 minutes on each side or until tender.
2. Meanwhile, heat a large nonstick skillet over medium-high heat, add sausage, and cook 3 minutes or until browned, breaking up larger pieces while cooking. Set aside on separate plate.
3. Add 2 cups water and the farro to any pan residue in skillet, bring to a boil, reduce heat to medium-low, cover, and simmer 15 minutes or until slightly "chewy." Stir in the sausage and cheese; cook, uncovered, for 2 minutes to thicken slightly. Spoon equal amounts into each mushroom cap and sprinkle with black pepper.

Nutrition Info: 200 cal., 6g fat (1g sag. fat), 30mg chol, 390mg sod., 23g carb (2g sugars, 3g fiber), 16g pro.

Avocado And Green Chili Chicken

Servings: 4
Cooking Time: 22 Minutes

Ingredients:
- 4 (4 ounces each) boneless, skinless chicken breast, flattened to 1/2-inch thickness
- 1 (4-ounce) can chopped mild green chilies
- 1 ripe medium avocado, chopped
- 1 lime, halved

Directions:
1. Preheat oven to 400°F.

2. Place chicken in an 11 × 7-inch baking pan, squeeze half of the lime over all. Spoon green chilies on top of each breast and spread over all. Bake, uncovered, 22–25 minutes or until chicken is no longer pink in center.

3. Top with avocado, squeeze remaining lime half over all, and sprinkle evenly with 1/4 teaspoon salt and 1/4 teaspoon pepper.

Nutrition Info: 200 cal., 8g fat (1g sag. fat), 85mg chol, 310mg sod., 6g carb (1g sugars, 3g fiber), 27g pro.

Cheesy Chicken And Rice

Servings: 4
Cooking Time: 12 Minutes

Ingredients:
- 1 1/2 cups water
- 1 cup instant brown rice
- 12 ounces frozen broccoli and cauliflower florets
- 12 ounces boneless, skinless chicken breast, rinsed and patted dry, cut into bite-sized pieces
- 3 ounces reduced-fat processed cheese (such as Velveeta), cut in 1/2-inch cubes

Directions:
1. Bring the water to boil in a large saucepan, then add the rice and vegetables. Return to a boil, reduce the heat, cover tightly, and simmer 10 minutes or until the liquid is absorbed.

2. Meanwhile, place a large nonstick skillet over medium heat until hot. Coat the skillet with nonstick cooking spray and add the chicken. Cook 10 minutes or until the chicken is no longer pink in the center and is just beginning to lightly brown on the edges, stirring frequently.

3. Add the chicken, cheese, 1/8 teaspoon salt, if desired, and pepper to the rice mixture and stir until the cheese has melted. Add pepper to taste, if desired.

Nutrition Info: 340 cal., 6g fat (1g sag. fat), 55mg chol, 380mg sod., 43g carb (4g sugars, 4g fiber), 28g pro.

Peach Barbecued Chicken

Servings: 4

Cooking Time: 18 Minutes

Ingredients:
- 8 chicken drumsticks, skin removed, rinsed and patted dry (about 2 pounds total)
- 2 tablespoons peach all-fruit spread
- 1/4 cup barbeque sauce, preferably hickory- or mesquite-flavored
- 2 teaspoons grated gingerroot

Directions:
1. Preheat the broiler.
2. Coat a broiler rack and pan with nonstick cooking spray. Arrange the drumsticks on the rack and broil about 4 inches away from heat source for 8 minutes. Turn and broil 6 minutes or until the juices run clear.
3. Meanwhile, place the fruit spread in a small glass bowl and microwave on HIGH 20 seconds or until the fruit spread has melted slightly. Add the barbeque sauce and ginger and stir to blend. Place 1 tablespoon of the mixture in a separate small bowl and set aside.
4. When the chicken is cooked, brush with half of the sauce and broil 2 minutes. Turn the drumsticks, brush with the remaining half of the sauce, and broil 2 more minutes.
5. Remove the drumsticks from the broiler, turn them over, and brush with the reserved 1 tablespoon sauce to serve.

Nutrition Info: 230 cal., 6g fat (1g sag. fat), 95mg chol, 220mg sod., 13g carb (10g sugars, 0g fiber), 29g pro.

POULTRY RECIPES

Panko Ranch Chicken Strips With Dipping Sauce

Servings: 4

Cooking Time: 12 Minutes

Ingredients:

- 8 chicken tenderloins, about 1 pound total
- 3/4 cup yogurt ranch dressing, divided use
- 3/4 cup panko breadcrumbs
- 3 tablespoons canola oil

Directions:

1. Place chicken in a medium bowl with 1/4 cup of the ranch dressing; toss until well coated. Place the breadcrumbs in a shallow pan, such as a pie pan. Coat chicken pieces, one at a time with the breadcrumbs and set aside.

2. Heat oil in a large skillet over medium-high heat. Add the chicken and immediately reduce to medium-low heat, cook 12 minutes or until golden and no longer pink in center, gently turning occasionally.

3. Remove from skillet, sprinkle with 1/8 teaspoon salt. Serve with remaining 1/2 cup ranch for dipping.

Nutrition Info: 340 cal., 16g fat (2g sag. fat), 85mg chol, 390mg sod., 17g carb (4g sugars, 1g fiber), 30g pro.

Molasses Drumsticks With Soy Sauce

Servings: 4

Cooking Time: 25 Minutes

Ingredients:

- 2 1/2 tablespoons lite soy sauce
- 1 1/4 tablespoons lime juice
- 8 chicken drumsticks, skin removed, rinsed, and patted dry
- 2 tablespoons dark molasses

Directions:

1. Stir the soy sauce and lime juice together in a small bowl until well blended.

2. Place the drumsticks in a large zippered plastic bag. Add 2 tablespoons of the soy sauce mixture to the bag. Seal tightly and shake back and forth to coat chicken evenly. Refrigerate overnight or at least 2 hours, turning occasionally.

3. Add the molasses to the remaining soy sauce mixture, cover with plastic wrap, and refrigerate until needed.

4. Preheat the broiler. Lightly coat the broiler rack and pan with nonstick cooking spray, place the drumsticks on the rack, and discard any marinade in the bag. Broil 6 inches away from the heat source for 25 minutes, turning every 5 minutes or until the drumsticks are no longer pink in the center.

5. Place the drumsticks in a large bowl. Stir the reserved soy sauce mixture and pour it over the drumsticks. Toss the drumsticks gently to coat evenly and let them stand 3 minutes to develop flavors.

Nutrition Info: 210 cal., 6g fat (1g sag. fat), 95mg chol, 450mg sod., 6g carb (4g sugars, 0g fiber), 30g pro.

Turkey Patties With Dark Onion Gravy

Servings: 4
Cooking Time: 20 Minutes

Ingredients:
- 1 pound 93% lean ground turkey
- 1 tablespoon flour
- 1 1/3 cups chopped yellow onion
- 1 tablespoon sodium-free chicken bouillon granules

Directions:
1. Shape the turkey into 4 patties, about 1/2 inch thick; sprinkle with 1/8 teaspoon salt and 1/8 teaspoon pepper, if desired.

2. Heat a large skillet over medium-high heat. Add flour and cook 3 minutes or until beginning to lightly brown, stirring constantly. Set aside on separate plate.

3. Coat skillet with cooking spray, add onions, and cook 3 minutes or until beginning to brown on edges. Push to one side of the skillet, add the turkey patties, reduce to medium heat, and cook 6 minutes on each side or until no longer pink in center.

4. Remove the turkey patties from the onion mixture and set aside on serving platter. Add 1 cup water and bouillon granules to the onions, sprinkle with the flour and 1/8 teaspoon salt and 1/8 teaspoon pepper. Stir and cook until thickened, about 1 1/2 to 2 minutes. Spoon over patties.

Nutrition Info: 210 cal., 10g fat (2g sag. fat), 84mg chol, 230mg sod., 8g carb (2g sugars, 1g fiber), 22g pro.

In-a-Pinch Chicken & Spinach

Servings: 4

Cooking Time: 25 Minutes

Ingredients:
- 4 boneless skinless chicken breast halves (6 ounces each)
- 2 tablespoons olive oil
- 1 tablespoon butter
- 1 package (6 ounces) fresh baby spinach
- 1 cup salsa

Directions:

1. Pound chicken with a meat mallet to 1/2-in. thickness. In a large skillet, heat oil and butter over medium heat. Cook the chicken for 5-6 minutes on each side or until no longer pink. Remove chicken and keep warm.

2. Add spinach and salsa to pan; cook and stir 3-4 minutes or just until spinach is wilted. Serve with chicken.

Nutrition Info: 297 cal., 14g fat (4g sat. fat), 102mg chol., 376mg sod., 6g carb. (2g sugars, 1g fiber), 36g pro.

POULTRY RECIPES

Turkey & Apricot Wraps

Servings: 4   Cooking Time: 15 Minutes

Ingredients:
- 1/2 cup reduced-fat cream cheese
- 3 tablespoons apricot preserves
- 4 whole wheat tortillas (8 inches), room temperature
- 1/2 pound sliced reduced-sodium deli turkey
- 2 cups fresh baby spinach or arugula

Directions:
1. In a small bowl, mix cream cheese and preserves. Spread about 2 tablespoons over each tortilla to within 1/2 in. of edges. Layer with turkey and spinach. Roll up tightly. Serve immediately or wrap in plastic wrap and refrigerate until serving.

Nutrition Info: 312 cal., 10g fat (4g sat. fat), 41mg chol., 655mg sod., 33g carb. (8g sugars, 2g fiber), 20g pro.

Rustic Mexican Chicken And Rice

Servings: 4
Cooking Time: 8 Hours

Ingredients:
- 1 pound boneless, skinless chicken thighs, trimmed of fat
- 1 (10-ounce) can diced tomatoes with green chilies
- 3/4 cup instant brown rice
- 2 tablespoons extra-virgin olive oil

Directions:
1. Combine chicken and tomatoes in a 3 1/2 to 4-quart slow cooker, cover, and cook on low setting for 7–8 hours or on high setting for 3 1/2–4 hours.
2. Gently stir in rice and 3/4 cup hot water, cover, and cook on high for 20 minutes.
3. Drizzle oil evenly over all and sprinkle with 1/8 teaspoon salt.

Nutrition Info: 250 cal., 12g fat (2g sag. fat), 110mg chol, 510mg sod., 12g carb (0g sugars, 1g fiber), 24g pro.

APPETIZERS AND SNACKS

Mocha Pumpkin Seeds

Servings: 3

Cooking Time: 25 Minutes

Ingredients:

- 6 tablespoons sugar
- 2 tablespoons baking cocoa
- 1 tablespoon instant coffee granules
- 1 large egg white
- 2 cups salted shelled pumpkin seeds (pepitas)

Directions:

1. Preheat oven to 325°. Place sugar, cocoa and coffee granules in a small food processor; cover and pulse until finely ground.
2. In a bowl, whisk egg white until frothy. Stir in pumpkin seeds. Sprinkle with sugar mixture; toss to coat evenly. Spread in a single layer in a parchment paper-lined 15x10x1-in. baking pan.
3. Bake 20-25 minutes or until dry and no longer sticky, stirring seeds every 10 minutes. Cool completely in pan. Store in an airtight container.

Nutrition Info: 142 cal., 10g fat (2g sat. fat), 0 chol., 55mg sod., 10g carb. (7g sugars, 1g fiber), 6g pro.

Basil Spread And Water Crackers

Servings: 4

Cooking Time: 5 Minutes

Ingredients:

- 2 ounces reduced-fat garlic and herb cream cheese
- 1/2 cup finely chopped fresh basil
- 12 fat-free water crackers

Directions:

1. Stir the cream cheese and basil together in a small bowl until well blended.
2. Place 1 teaspoon spread on each cracker.

Nutrition Info: 70 cal., 2g fat (1g sag. fat), 0mg chol, 200mg sod., 9g carb (1g sugars, 0g fiber), 3g pro.

Crostini With Kalamata Tomato

Servings: 4
Cooking Time: 10 Minutes

Ingredients:
- 4 ounces multigrain baguette bread, cut in 12 slices (about 1/4 inch thick)
- 1 small tomato, finely chopped
- 9 small kalamata olives, pitted and finely chopped
- 2 tablespoons chopped fresh basil

Directions:
1. Preheat the oven to 350°F.
2. Arrange the bread slices on a baking sheet and bake 10 minutes or until just golden on the edges. Remove from the heat and cool completely.
3. Meanwhile, stir the remaining ingredients together in a small bowl. Spread 1 tablespoon of the mixture on each bread slice.

Nutrition Info: 90 cal., 2g fat (0g sag. fat), 0mg chol, 220mg sod., 16g carb (2g sugars, 1g fiber), 3g pro.

APPETIZERS AND SNACKS

Lime'd Blueberries

Servings: 6
Cooking Time: 5 Minutes

Ingredients:

- 2 cups frozen unsweetened blueberries, partially thawed
- 1/4 cup frozen grape juice concentrate
- 1 1/2 tablespoons lime juice

Directions:

1. Place all ingredients in a medium bowl and toss gently.
2. Serve immediately for peak flavor and texture.

Nutrition Info: 50 cal., 0g fat (0g sag. fat), 0mg chol, 5mg sod., 13g carb (11g sugars, 1g fiber), 0g pro.

Bleu Cheese'd Pears

Servings: 4
Cooking Time: 5 Minutes

Ingredients:

- 2 ounces fat-free cream cheese
- 3 1/2 tablespoons crumbled bleu cheese
- 2 medium firm pears, halved, cored, and sliced into 20 slices

Directions:

1. In a small bowl, microwave the cheeses on HIGH for 10 seconds to soften. Use a rubber spatula to blend well.
2. Top each pear slice with 3/4 teaspoon cheese.
3. To prevent the pear slices from discoloring, toss them with a tablespoon of orange, pineapple, or lemon juice. Shake off the excess liquid before topping them with cheese.

Nutrition Info: 90 cal., 2g fat (1g sag. fat), 10mg chol, 190mg sod., 14g carb (9g sugars, 3g fiber), 4g pro.

Tuna Salad Stuffed Eggs

Servings: 4

Cooking Time: 10 Minutes

Ingredients:
- 4 large eggs
- 1 (2.6-ounce) packet tuna (or 5-ounce can of tuna packed in water, rinsed and well drained)
- 2 tablespoons reduced-fat mayonnaise
- 1 1/2–2 tablespoons sweet pickle relish

Directions:

1. Place eggs in a medium saucepan and cover with cold water. Bring to a boil over high heat, then reduce the heat and simmer 10 minutes.

2. Meanwhile, stir the tuna, mayonnaise, and relish together in a small bowl.

3. When the eggs are cooked, remove them from the water and let stand one minute before peeling under cold running water. Cut eggs in half, lengthwise, and discard 4 egg yolk halves and place the other 2 egg yolk halves in the tuna mixture and stir with a rubber spatula until well blended. Spoon equal amounts of the tuna mixture in each of the egg halves.

4. Serve immediately, or cover with plastic wrap and refrigerate up to 24 hours.

Nutrition Info: 90 cal., 4g fat (1g sag. fat), 105mg chol, 240mg sod., 3g carb (2g sugars, 0g fiber), 9g pro.

APPETIZERS AND SNACKS

Dilled Chex Toss

Servings: 18   Cooking Time: 30 Minutes

Ingredients:
- 6 cups multi-grain or Wheat Chex cereal
- 4-ounce packet ranch salad dressing mix
- 1 tablespoon dried dill
- 2 tablespoons extra virgin olive oil

Directions:

1. Preheat the oven to 175°F.
2. Place the cereal, dressing mix, and dill in a large zippered plastic bag. Seal and shake gently to blend well.
3. Place the mixture on a large rimmed baking sheet or jelly roll pan, drizzle the oil evenly over all, and stir thoroughly to blend. Spread out in a single layer and bake 30 minutes or until browned lightly, stirring once.

Nutrition Info: 50 cal., 1g fat (0g sag. fat), 0mg chol, 200mg sod., 8g carb (1g sugars, 1g fiber), 1g pro.

Creamy Apricot Fruit Dip

Servings: 4

Cooking Time: 5 Minutes

Ingredients:
- 1/3 cup fat-free vanilla-flavored yogurt
- 1/4 cup fat-free whipped topping
- 2 tablespoons apricot all-fruit spread
- 2 cups whole strawberries or 2 medium apples, halved, cored, and sliced

Directions:

1. In a small bowl, whisk the yogurt, whipped topping, and fruit spread until well blended.
2. Serve with fruit.

Nutrition Info: 60 cal., 0g fat (0g sag. fat), 0mg chol, 15mg sod., 14g carb (9g sugars, 2g fiber), 1g pro.

Minutesi Feta Pizzas

Servings: 4
Cooking Time: 20 Minutes

Ingredients:
- 2 whole wheat English muffins, split and toasted
- 2 tablespoons reduced-fat cream cheese
- 4 teaspoons prepared pesto
- 1/2 cup thinly sliced red onion
- 1/4 cup crumbled feta cheese

Directions:
1. Preheat oven to 425°. Place muffins on a baking sheet.
2. Mix cream cheese and pesto; spread over muffins. Top with onion and feta cheese. Bake until lightly browned, 6-8 minutes.

Nutrition Info: 136 cal., 6g fat (3g sat. fat), 11mg chol., 294mg sod., 16g carb. (4g sugars, 3g fiber), 6g pro.

Balsamic-Goat Cheese Grilled Plums

Servings: 8
Cooking Time: 25 Minutes

Ingredients:
- 1 cup balsamic vinegar
- 2 teaspoons grated lemon peel
- 4 medium firm plums, halved and pitted
- 1/2 cup crumbled goat cheese

Directions:
1. For glaze, in a small saucepan, combine vinegar and lemon peel; bring to a boil. Cook 10-12 minutes or until mixture is thickened and reduced to about 1/3 cup (do not overcook).

APPETIZERS AND SNACKS

2. Grill plums, covered, over medium heat 2-3 minutes on each side or until tender. Drizzle with glaze; top with goat cheese.

Nutrition Info: 58 cal., 2g fat (1g sat. fat), 9mg chol., 41mg sod., 9g carb. (8g sugars, 1g fiber), 2g pro.

Sweet Peanut Buttery Dip

Servings: 4

Cooking Time: 5 Minutes

Ingredients:
- 1/3 cup fat-free vanilla-flavored yogurt
- 2 tablespoons reduced-fat peanut butter
- 2 teaspoons packed dark brown sugar
- 2 medium bananas, sliced

Directions:

1. Using a fork or whisk, stir the yogurt, peanut butter, and brown sugar together in a small bowl until completely blended.

2. Serve with banana slices and wooden toothpicks, if desired.

Nutrition Info: 120 cal., 3g fat (0g sag. fat), 0mg chol, 40mg sod., 21g carb (12g sugars, 2g fiber), 3g pro.

Baby Carrots And Spicy Cream Dip

Servings: 4

Cooking Time: 5 Minutes

Ingredients:
- 1/3 cup fat-free sour cream
- 3 tablespoons reduced-fat tub-style cream cheese
- 3/4 teaspoon hot pepper sauce
- 1/8 teaspoon salt
- 48 baby carrots

Directions:
1. Stir the sour cream, cream cheese, pepper sauce, and salt together until well blended.
2. Let stand at least 10 minutes to develop flavors and mellow slightly. Serve with carrots.

Nutrition Info: 90 cal., 2g fat (1g sag. fat), 10mg chol, 240mg sod., 16g carb (7g sugars, 3g fiber), 3g pro.

FISH & SEAFOOD RECIPES

Two-Sauce Cajun Fish

Servings: 4

Cooking Time: 12–15 Minutes

Ingredients:

- 4 (4-ounce) tilapia filets (or any mild, lean white fish filets), rinsed and patted dry
- 1/2 teaspoon seafood seasoning
- 1 (14.5-ounce) can stewed tomatoes with Cajun seasonings, well drained
- 2 tablespoons no-trans-fat margarine (35% vegetable oil)

Directions:

1. Preheat the oven to 400°F.
2. Coat a broiler rack and pan with nonstick cooking spray, arrange the fish filets on the rack about 2 inches apart, and sprinkle them evenly with the seafood seasoning.
3. Place the tomatoes in a blender and puree until just smooth. Set aside 1/4 cup of the mixture in a small glass bowl.
4. Spoon the remaining tomatoes evenly over the top of each filet and bake 12–15 minutes or until the filets are opaque in the center.
5. Meanwhile, add the margarine to the reserved 1/4 cup tomato mixture and microwave on HIGH 20 seconds or until the mixture is just melted. Stir to blend well.
6. Place the filets on a serving platter, spoon the tomato-margarine mixture over the center of each filet, and sprinkle each lightly with chopped fresh parsley, if desired.

Nutrition Info: 150 cal., 5g fat (1g sag. fat), 50mg chol, 250mg sod., 4g carb (3g sugars, 1g fiber), 23g pro.

FISH & SEAFOOD RECIPES

Pesto Grilled Salmon

Servings: 12
Cooking Time: 30 Minutes

Ingredients:
- 1 salmon fillet (3 pounds)
- 1/2 cup prepared pesto
- 2 green onions, finely chopped
- 1/4 cup lemon juice
- 2 garlic cloves, minced

Directions:

1. Moisten a paper towel with cooking oil; using long-handled tongs, lightly coat the grill rack. Place salmon skin side down on grill rack. Grill, covered, over medium heat or broil 4 in. from the heat for 5 minutes.

2. In a small bowl, combine the pesto, onions, lemon juice and garlic. Carefully spoon some of the pesto mixture over salmon. Grill for about 15-20 minutes longer or until the fish flakes easily with a fork, basting occasionally with the remaining pesto mixture.

Nutrition Info: 262 cal., 17g fat (4g sat. fat), 70mg chol., 147mg sod., 1g carb. (0 sugars, 0 fiber), 25g pro.

Shrimp And Noodles Parmesan

Servings: 4

Cooking Time: 10 Minutes

Ingredients:
- 8 ounces uncooked whole-wheat no-yolk egg noodles
- 1 pound peeled raw shrimp, rinsed and patted dry
- 1/4 cup no-trans-fat margarine (35% vegetable oil)
- 1/4 teaspoon salt
- 3 tablespoons grated fresh Parmesan cheese

Directions:

1. Cook noodles according to package directions, omitting any salt or fat.

2. Meanwhile, place a large nonstick skillet over medium heat until hot. Coat with nonstick cooking spray and sauté the shrimp for 4–5 minutes or until opaque in the center, stirring frequently.

3. Drain the noodles well in a colander and place in a pasta bowl. Add the margarine, shrimp, salt, and black pepper, to taste (if desired), and toss gently. Sprinkle evenly with the Parmesan cheese.

Nutrition Info: 340 cal., 7g fat (1g sag. fat), 190mg chol, 410mg sod., 42g carb (0g sugars, 6g fiber), 33g pro.

Lemony Steamed Spa Fish

Servings: 4

Cooking Time: 6 Minutes

Ingredients:

- 2 lemons, sliced into ¼-inch-thick rounds, plus lemon wedges for serving
- 4 (6-ounce) sole fillets, ¼ to ½ inch thick
- ¼ teaspoon salt
- ⅛ teaspoon pepper
- 1 tablespoon minced fresh chives, tarragon, cilantro, basil, or parsley

Directions:

1. Place steamer basket in Dutch oven and add water until it just touches bottom of basket. Line basket with half of lemon slices, cover pot, and bring water to boil over high heat. Meanwhile, pat sole dry with paper towels, sprinkle with salt and pepper, and roll each fillet into bundle.

2. Reduce heat to medium-low and bring water to simmer. Lay fish bundles in basket, seam-side down, and top with remaining lemon slices. Cover pot and steam until sole flakes apart when gently prodded with paring knife, 4 to 6 minutes.

3. Gently transfer fish bundles to individual serving plates (discarding lemon slices), sprinkle with herbs, and serve with lemon wedges.

Nutrition Info: 120 cal., 3g fat (1g sag. fat), 75mg chol, 280mg sod., 0g carb (0g sugars, 0g fiber), 21g pro.

Salmon With Lemon-Thyme Slices

Servings: 4

Cooking Time: 10–12 Minutes

Ingredients:

- 2 medium lemons
- 4 (4-ounce) salmon filets, rinsed and patted dry, skinned (if desired)
- 1/2 teaspoon dried thyme, crushed
- 1/4 teaspoon salt
- 1/4 teaspoon black pepper

Directions:

1. Preheat the oven to 400°F.
2. Line a baking sheet with foil and coat with nonstick cooking spray. Slice one of the lemons into 8 rounds and arrange on the baking sheet.
3. Place the salmon on top of the lemon slices, spray the salmon lightly with nonstick cooking spray, and sprinkle evenly with the thyme, salt, and pepper. Bake the salmon 10–12 minutes or until it flakes with a fork.
4. Cut the other lemon in quarters and squeeze lemon juice evenly over all.

Nutrition Info: 180 cal., 9g fat (1g sag. fat), 60mg chol, 220mg sod., 3g carb (1g sugars, 1g fiber), 22g pro.

Pan-Seared Sesame-Crusted Tuna Steaks

Servings: 4

Cooking Time: 8 Minutes

Ingredients:
- ¾ cup sesame seeds
- 4 (6-ounce) skinless tuna steaks, 1 inch thick
- 2 tablespoons canola oil
- ¼ teaspoon salt
- ⅛ teaspoon pepper

Directions:
1. Spread sesame seeds in shallow baking dish. Pat tuna steaks dry with paper towels, rub steaks all over with 1 tablespoon oil, then sprinkle with salt and pepper. Press both sides of each steak in sesame seeds to coat.

2. Heat remaining 1 tablespoon oil in 12-inch nonstick skillet over medium-high heat until just smoking. Place steaks in skillet and cook until seeds are golden and tuna is translucent red at center when checked with tip of paring knife and registers 110 degrees (for rare), 1 to 2 minutes per side. Transfer tuna to cutting board and slice ½ inch thick. Serve.

Nutrition Info: 330 cal., 15g fat (1g sag. fat), 65mg chol, 250mg sod., 2g carb (0g sugars, 1g fiber), 45g pro.

FISH & SEAFOOD RECIPES

Buttery Lemon Grilled Fish On Grilled Asparagus

Servings: 4
Cooking Time: 12 Minutes

Ingredients:
- 1 pound asparagus spears, ends trimmed
- 4 (4-ounce) cod filets, rinsed and patted dry
- Juice and zest of a medium lemon
- 1/4 cup light butter with canola oil

Directions:

1. Heat a grill or grill pan over medium-high heat. Coat the asparagus with cooking spray and cook 6–8 minutes or until just tender-crisp, turning occasionally. Set aside on a rimmed serving platter and cover to keep warm.

2. Coat both sides of the fish with cooking spray, sprinkle with 1/4 teaspoon black pepper, if desired, and cook 3 minutes on each side or until opaque in center.

3. Meanwhile, combine the light butter, lemon zest and 1/4 teaspoon salt, if desired, in a small bowl.

4. Spoon the butter mixture over the asparagus and spread over all. Top with the fish and squeeze lemon juice over fish.

Nutrition Info: 160 cal., 6g fat (1g sag. fat), 50mg chol, 210mg sod., 6g carb (3g sugars, 3g fiber), 23g pro.

Teriyaki Salmon

Servings: 4

Cooking Time: 30 Minutes

Ingredients:
- 3/4 cup reduced-sodium teriyaki sauce
- 1/2 cup maple syrup
- 4 salmon fillets (6 ounces each)
- Mixed salad greens, optional

Directions:

1. In a small bowl, whisk teriyaki sauce and syrup. Pour 1 cup marinade into a large resealable plastic bag. Add salmon; seal bag and turn to coat. Refrigerate 15 minutes. Cover and refrigerate any of the remaining marinade.

2. Drain the salmon, discarding the marinade in bag. Moisten a paper towel with cooking oil; using long-handled tongs, rub on grill rack to coat lightly.

3. Place salmon on grill rack, skin side down. Grill, covered, over medium heat or broil 4 in. from heat 8-12 minutes or until fish just begins to flake easily with a fork, basting frequently with reserved marinade. If desired, serve over mixed salad greens.

Nutrition Info: 362 cal., 18g fat (4g sat. fat), 100mg chol., 422mg sod., 12g carb. (12g sugars, 0 fiber), 35g pro.

No-Fry Fish Fry

Servings: 4

Cooking Time: 6 Minutes

Ingredients:
- 2 tablespoons yellow cornmeal
- 2 teaspoons Cajun seasoning
- 4 (4-ounce) tilapia filets (or any mild, lean white fish filets), rinsed and patted dry
- 1/8 teaspoon salt
- Lemon wedges (optional)

Directions:
1. Preheat the broiler.
2. Coat a broiler rack and pan with nonstick cooking spray and set aside.
3. Mix the cornmeal and Cajun seasoning thoroughly in a shallow pan, such as a pie plate. Coat each filet with nonstick cooking spray and coat evenly with the cornmeal mixture.
4. Place the filets on the rack and broil 6 inches away from the heat source for 3 minutes on each side.
5. Place the filets on a serving platter, sprinkle each evenly with salt, and serve with lemon wedges, if desired.

Nutrition Info: 130 cal., 2g fat (0g sag. fat), 50mg chol, 250mg sod., 4g carb (0g sugars, 0g fiber), 23g pro.

Oven-Roasted Salmon

Servings: 4

Cooking Time: 10 Minutes

Ingredients:
- 1 (1½-pound) skin-on salmon fillet, 1 inch thick
- 1 teaspoon extra-virgin olive oil
- ¼ teaspoon salt
- ⅛ teaspoon pepper

Directions:

1. Adjust oven rack to lowest position, place aluminum foil–lined rimmed baking sheet on rack, and heat oven to 500 degrees. Cut salmon crosswise into 4 fillets, then make 4 or 5 shallow slashes about an inch apart along skin side of each piece, being careful not to cut into flesh. Pat fillets dry with paper towels, rub with oil, and sprinkle with salt and pepper.

2. Once oven reaches 500 degrees, reduce oven temperature to 275 degrees. Remove sheet from oven and carefully place salmon, skin-side down, on hot sheet. Roast until centers are still translucent when checked with tip of paring knife and register 125 degrees (for medium-rare), 4 to 6 minutes.

3. Slide spatula along underside of fillets and transfer to individual serving plates or serving platter, leaving skin behind; discard skin. Serve.

Nutrition Info: 360 cal., 24g fat (5g sag. fat), 95mg chol, 250mg sod., 0g carb (0g sugars, 0g fiber), 35g pro.

VEGETABLES, FRUIT AND SIDE DISHES

Roasted Spiralized Carrots

Servings: 6

Cooking Time: 15 Minutes

Ingredients:
- 2 pounds carrots, trimmed and peeled
- 2 tablespoons extra-virgin olive oil
- 2 teaspoons minced fresh thyme
- Salt and pepper

Directions:

1. Adjust oven rack to middle position and heat oven to 375 degrees. Using spiralizer, cut carrots into ⅛-inch-thick noodles, then cut noodles into 12-inch lengths. Toss carrots with 1 tablespoon oil, thyme, ½ teaspoon salt, and ¼ teaspoon pepper on rimmed baking sheet. Cover baking sheet tightly with aluminum foil and roast for 15 minutes. Remove foil and continue to roast until carrots are tender, 10 to 15 minutes.

2. Transfer carrots to serving platter, drizzle with remaining 1 tablespoon oil, and season with pepper to taste. Serve.

Nutrition Info: 100 cal., 5g fat (0g sag. fat), 0mg chol, 290mg sod., 13g carb (6g sugars, 4g fiber), 1g pro.

Creole-Simmered Vegetables

Servings: 4

Cooking Time: 24 Minutes

Ingredients:
- 1 (14.5-ounce) can stewed tomatoes with Cajun seasonings
- 2 cups frozen pepper and onion stir-fry
- 3/4 cup thinly sliced celery
- 1 tablespoon no-trans-fat margarine (35% vegetable oil)

Directions:

1. Place all the ingredients except the margarine in a medium saucepan and bring to a boil over high heat. Reduce the heat, cover tightly, and simmer 20 minutes or until the onions are very tender.

2. Increase the heat to high and cook 2 minutes, uncovered, to thicken the vegetables slightly. Remove from the heat and stir in the margarine.

Nutrition Info: 60 cal., 1g fat (0g sag. fat), 0mg chol, 210mg sod., 10g carb (6g sugars, 2g fiber), 2g pro.

Saucy Eggplant And Capers

Servings: 4

Cooking Time: 21 Minutes

Ingredients:
- 10 ounces eggplant, diced (about 2 1/2 cups)
- 1 (14.5-ounce) can stewed tomatoes with Italian seasonings
- 2 tablespoons chopped fresh basil
- 2 teaspoons capers, drained
- 2 teaspoons extra virgin olive oil (optional)

Directions:

1. Bring the eggplant and tomatoes to boil in a large saucepan over high heat. Reduce the heat, cover tightly, and simmer 20 minutes or until the eggplant is very tender.

2. Remove the saucepan from the heat, stir in the basil, capers, and 2 teaspoons extra virgin olive oil (if desired), and let stand 3 minutes to develop flavors.

Nutrition Info: 50 cal., 0g fat (0g sag. fat), 0mg chol, 250mg sod., 12g carb (7g sugars, 3g fiber), 2g pro.

Roasted Beets

Servings: 4
Cooking Time: 60 Minutes

Ingredients:
- 1½ pounds beets, trimmed
- 1 tablespoon extra-virgin olive oil
- 1 tablespoon sherry vinegar
- 1 tablespoon minced fresh parsley
- Salt and pepper

Directions:

1. Adjust oven rack to middle position and heat oven to 400 degrees. Wrap beets individually in aluminum foil and place on rimmed baking sheet. Roast beets until skewer inserted into center meets little resistance (you will need to unwrap beets to test them), 45 to 60 minutes.

2. Remove beets from oven and slowly open foil packets (being careful of rising steam). When beets are cool enough to handle but still warm, gently rub off skins using paper towels.

3. Slice beets into ½-inch-thick wedges, then toss with oil, vinegar, parsley, and ¼ teaspoon salt. Season with pepper to taste and serve warm or at room temperature. (Beets can be refrigerated for up to 3 days; return to room temperature before serving.)

Nutrition Info: 80 cal., 3g fat (0g sag. fat), 0mg chol, 240mg sod., 11g carb (8g sugars, 3g fiber), 2g pro.

VEGETABLES, FRUIT AND SIDE DISHES

Roasted Beans And Green Onions

Servings: 4

Cooking Time: 11 Minutes

Ingredients:

- 8 ounces green string beans, trimmed
- 4 whole green onions, trimmed and cut in fourths (about 3-inch pieces)
- 1 1/2 teaspoons extra virgin olive oil
- 1/4 teaspoon salt

Directions:

1. Preheat the oven to 425°F.
2. Line a baking sheet with foil and coat the foil with nonstick cooking spray.
3. Toss the beans, onions, and oil together in a medium bowl. Arrange them in a thin layer on the baking sheet.
4. Bake for 8 minutes and stir gently, using two utensils as you would for a stir-fry. Bake another 3–4 minutes or until the beans begin to brown on the edges and are tender-crisp.
5. Remove the pan from the oven and sprinkle the beans with salt.

Nutrition Info: 35 cal., 2g fat (0g sag. fat), 0mg chol, 150mg sod., 5g carb (1g sugars, 2g fiber), 1g pro.

VEGETABLES, FRUIT AND SIDE DISHES

Best Baked Sweet Potatoes

Servings:4

Cooking Time:8minutes

Ingredients:

- 4 (8-ounce) sweet potatoes, unpeeled, each lightly pricked with fork in 3 places

Directions:

1. Adjust oven rack to middle position and heat oven to 425 degrees. Place wire rack in aluminum foil–lined rimmed baking sheet and spray rack with vegetable oil spray. Place potatoes on large plate and microwave until potatoes yield to gentle pressure and reach internal temperature of 200 degrees, 6 to 9 minutes, flipping potatoes every 3 minutes.

2. Transfer potatoes to prepared rack and bake for 1 hour (exteriors of potatoes will be lightly browned and potatoes will feel very soft when squeezed).

3. Slit each potato lengthwise; using clean dish towel, hold ends and squeeze slightly to push flesh up and out. Transfer potatoes to serving dish. Serve.

Nutrition Info: 170 cal., 0g fat (0g sag. fat), 0mg chol, 120mg sod., 40g carb (12g sugars, 7g fiber), 3g pro.

VEGETABLES, FRUIT AND SIDE DISHES

Buttery Tarragon Sugar Snaps

Servings: 4   Cooking Time: 8 Minutes

Ingredients:
- 8 ounces sugar snap peas, trimmed
- 1 1/2 tablespoons no-trans-fat margarine (35% vegetable oil)
- 1 tablespoon chopped fresh parsley
- 1/2 teaspoon dried tarragon
- 1/4 teaspoon salt

Directions:
1. Steam the sugar snaps for 6 minutes or until they are tender-crisp.
2. Place them in a serving bowl, add the remaining ingredients, and toss gently.

Nutrition Info: 45 cal., 2g fat (0g sag. fat), 0mg chol, 180mg sod., 5g carb (2g sugars, 1g fiber), 1g pro.

Light Glazed Skillet Apples

Servings: 4   Cooking Time: 5 Minutes

Ingredients:
- 1 tablespoon no-trans-fat margarine
- 1/2 tablespoon sugar
- 2 cups Granny Smith apple slices

Directions:
1. Melt the margarine in a large skillet over medium heat, then tilt the skillet to coat the bottom evenly. Sprinkle the sugar evenly over the skillet bottom.
2. Arrange the apples in a single layer on top of the sugar. Cook 1–1 1/2 minutes or until the apples just begin to turn golden. Do not stir.
3. Using two forks or a spoon and a fork for easy handling, turn the apple slices over and cook 1 minute. Continue to cook and turn again until the apples are golden on both sides, about 2 minutes longer.

Nutrition Info: 45 cal., 1g fat (0g sag. fat), 0mg chol, 20mg sod., 9g carb (7g sugars, 1g fiber), 0g pro.

VEGETABLES, FRUIT AND SIDE DISHES

Pan-Roasted Broccoli

Servings: 6

Cooking Time: 10 minutes

Ingredients:

- ¼ teaspoon salt
- ⅛ teaspoon pepper
- 2 tablespoons extra-virgin olive oil
- 1¾ pounds broccoli, florets cut into 1½-inch pieces, stalks peeled and cut on bias into ¼-inch-thick slices

Directions:

1. Stir 3 tablespoons water, salt, and pepper together in small bowl until salt dissolves; set aside. Heat oil in 12-inch nonstick skillet over medium-high heat until just smoking. Add broccoli stalks in even layer and cook, without stirring, until browned on bottoms, about 2 minutes. Add florets to skillet and toss to combine. Cook, without stirring, until bottoms of florets just begin to brown, 1 to 2 minutes.

2. Add water mixture and cover skillet. Cook until broccoli is bright green but still crisp, about 2 minutes. Uncover and continue to cook until water has evaporated, broccoli stalks are tender, and florets are crisp-tender, about 2 minutes. Serve.

Nutrition Info: 70 cal., 5g fat (0g sag. fat), 0mg chol, 125mg sod., 5g carb (1g sugars, 2g fiber), 2g pro.

VEGETABLES, FRUIT AND SIDE DISHES

Roasted Asparagus

Servings: 6

Cooking Time: 10 Minutes

Ingredients:
- 2 pounds thick asparagus, trimmed
- 2 tablespoons plus 2 teaspoons extra-virgin olive oil
- ½ teaspoon salt
- ¼ teaspoon pepper

Directions:

1. Adjust oven rack to lowest position, place rimmed baking sheet on rack, and heat oven to 500 degrees. Peel bottom halves of asparagus spears until white flesh is exposed, then toss with 2 tablespoons oil, salt, and pepper.

2. Transfer asparagus to preheated sheet and spread into single layer. Roast, without moving asparagus, until undersides of spears are browned, tops are bright green, and tip of paring knife inserted at base of largest spear meets little resistance, 8 to 10 minutes. Transfer asparagus to serving platter and drizzle with remaining 2 teaspoons oil. Serve.

Nutrition Info: 80 cal., 6g fat (1g sag. fat), 0mg chol, 190mg sod., 4g carb (2g sugars, 2g fiber), 3g pro.

Slow-Cooked Whole Carrots

Servings: 6

Cooking Time: 45 Minutes

Ingredients:
- 1 tablespoon extra-virgin olive oil
- ½ teaspoon salt
- 1½ pounds carrots, peeled

Directions:
1. Cut parchment paper into 11-inch circle, then cut 1-inch hole in center, folding paper as needed.
2. Bring 3 cups water, oil, and salt to simmer in 12-inch skillet over high heat. Off heat, add carrots, top with parchment, cover skillet, and let sit for 20 minutes.
3. Uncover, leaving parchment in place, and bring to simmer over high heat. Reduce heat to medium-low and cook until most of water has evaporated and carrots are very tender, about 45 minutes.
4. Discard parchment, increase heat to medium-high, and cook, shaking skillet often, until carrots are lightly glazed and no water remains, 2 to 4 minutes. Serve.

Nutrition Info: 60 cal., 2g fat (0g sag. fat), 0mg chol, 100mg sod., 10g carb (5g sugars, 3g fiber), 1g pro.

VEGETABLES, FRUIT AND SIDE DISHES

Grilled Soy Pepper Petites

Servings: 4

Cooking Time: 12 Minutes

Ingredients:
- 1 pound petite peppers
- 3 tablespoons apricot or raspberry fruit spread
- 1 1/2 tablespoons light soy sauce
- 1/8 to 1/4 teaspoon dried pepper flakes

Directions:

1. Heat a grill or grill pan over medium-high heat. Coat peppers with cooking spray and cook 12 minutes or until tender and beginning to char, turning frequently.

2. Meanwhile, heat fruit spread in microwave for 15 seconds to melt slightly; whisk in soy sauce and pepper flakes.

3. Place peppers in a shallow bowl or rimmed platter and toss with mixture. Serve warm or room temperature.

Nutrition Info: 55 cal., 0g fat (0g sag. fat), 0mg chol, 200mg sod., 12g carb (9g sugars, 2g fiber), 2g pro.

Hot Skillet Pineapple

Servings: 4

Cooking Time: 7 Minutes

Ingredients:
- 2 tablespoons no-trans-fat margarine (35% vegetable oil)
- 1 1/2 teaspoons packed dark brown sugar
- 1/2 teaspoon ground curry powder
- 8 slices pineapple packed in juice

Directions:

1. Place a large nonstick skillet over medium-high heat until hot. Add the margarine, sugar, and curry and bring to a boil. Stir to blend.

2. Arrange the pineapple slices in a single layer in the skillet. Cook 6 minutes until the pineapples are richly golden in color, turning frequently.

3. Arrange the pineapples on a serving platter and let stand 5 minutes to develop flavors and cool slightly. Serve hot or room temperature.

Nutrition Info: 70 cal., 2g fat (0g sag. fat), 0mg chol, 45mg sod., 13g carb (12g sugars, 1g fiber), 0g pro.

VEGETABLES, FRUIT AND SIDE DISHES

Broccoli Piquant

Servings: 4

Cooking Time: 7 Minutes

Ingredients:

- 10 ounces fresh broccoli florets
- 1 tablespoon no-trans-fat margarine (35% vegetable oil)
- 1 teaspoon Worcestershire sauce
- 1 teaspoon lemon juice
- 1/4 teaspoon salt

Directions:

1. Steam the broccoli for 6 minutes or until the broccoli is tender-crisp.
2. Meanwhile, microwave the remaining ingredients in a small glass bowl on HIGH for 15 seconds. Stir until smooth.
3. Place the broccoli on a serving platter and drizzle the sauce evenly over all.

Nutrition Info: 35 cal., 1g fat (0g sag. fat), 0mg chol, 200mg sod., 4g carb (2g sugars, 2g fiber), 2g pro.

Skillet-Roasted Veggies

Servings: 4

Cooking Time: 6 Minutes

Ingredients:
- 5 ounces asparagus spears, trimmed and cut into 2-inch pieces (1 cup total), patted dry
- 3 ounces sliced portobello mushrooms (1/2 of a 6-ounce package)
- 1/2 medium red bell pepper, cut in thin strips
- 1/4 teaspoon salt
- 1/8 teaspoon black pepper

Directions:

1. Place a large nonstick skillet over medium-high heat until hot. Coat the skillet with nonstick cooking spray and add the asparagus, mushrooms, and bell pepper. Coat the vegetables with nonstick cooking spray and sprinkle evenly with the salt and black pepper.

2. Cook 5–6 minutes, or until the vegetables begin to richly brown on the edges. Use two utensils to stir as you would when stir-frying.

3. Remove from the heat, cover tightly, and let stand 2 minutes to develop flavors.

Nutrition Info: 15 cal., 0g fat (0g sag. fat), 0mg chol, 150mg sod., 3g carb (1g sugars, 1g fiber), 1g pro.

Printed in Great Britain
by Amazon